The AskA Starter Kit:

How to Build and Maintain Digital Reference Services

by
R. David Lankes
Abby S. Kasowitz

November 1998

ERIC® Clearinghouse on Information & Technology
Syracuse University
Syracuse, New York
IR-107

UMass Dartmouth

The AskA Starter Kit: How to Build and Maintain Digital Reference Services

by R. David Lankes and Abby S. Kasowitz

This publication is available from Information Resources Publications, Syracuse University, 4-194 Center for Science and Technology, Syracuse, New York 13244-4100; 1-800-464-9107 (IR-107)

ISBN: 0-937597-47-3

U.S. Department of Education
Office of Educational Research and Improvement
National Library of Education

ERIC is a program administered by the National Library of Education, a unit of the Office of Educational Research and Improvement, U.S. Department of Education. This product was prepared under contract no. RR93002009. The content does not necessarily reflect the views of the Department or any other agency of the U.S. Government.

Eric Plotnick, Editor in Chief
Susann L. Wurster, Copy Editor
R.D. Lankes, Cover Design

About the Authors

R. David Lankes, Ph.D., is director of the ERIC Clearinghouse on Information & Technology at Syracuse University. He is co-founder of AskERIC, the award winning project that provides high-quality education information to educators via the Internet, and is founder of the Virtual Reference Desk project.

Dave is a faculty member for Syracuse University's School of Information Studies and he speaks and consults nationally on Internet issues in education and business. His work focuses on Internet information services and the increasing demands of users in the dynamic Internet environment. Dave earned his B.F.A. (Multimedia Design), M.S. in Telecommunications, and Ph.D. in Information Transfer from Syracuse University.

Abby S. Kasowitz is coordinator of the Virtual Reference Desk (VRD) Project at the Information Institute of Syracuse. She manages and participates in all aspects of the project including organizing stakeholders' meetings and digital reference workshops, consulting on AskA service development, designing software for digital reference, surveying digital reference services, writing instructional materials, and conducting presentations. Abby previously worked for the KidsConnect AskA service where she developed its volunteer training program, responded to queries of K-12 students and assisted in daily service operations.

Abby earned a B.A. in English and American Literature from Brandeis University. She received an M.S. in Instructional Design, Development and Evaluation and an M.L.S. from Syracuse University and is certified as a school library media specialist.

The AskA Starter Kit:
How to Build and Maintain Digital Reference Services

Condensed Table of Contents

The AskA Starter Kit: How to Build and Maintain Digital Reference Services

Expanded Table of Contents

List of Tables

List of Figures

List of Work Sheets

Case Studies

Acknowledgements

Many people were involved in shaping the Starter Kit through their ideas and experiences in digital reference service. The authors would like to thank everyone who participated in this endeavor through one-on-one discussions, e-mail correspondence, and writing of case studies that appear throughout the Starter Kit. A special thank you goes to Joann Wasik of the Virtual Reference Desk project for contributing various sections, reviewing the text, and providing moral support. Thanks to the following people who offered specific information on training programs and other aspects of AskA services: Ken Williams, The Math Forum; Lynn Bry, MAD Scientist Network; Blythe Bennett, KidsConnect; Robin Summers, former AskERIC Coordinator; Pauline Lynch, AskERIC; John Kosakowski, AskERIC; Bryan Blank and Lorri Mon, Internet Public Library; Joe Janes, Founding Director, Internet Public Library; Anton Ninno, AskERIC Digital Library Consultant; and Sten Odenwald, Raytheon STX Corporation.

Thanks to the Virtual Reference Desk Expert Panel members for beginning to set the standards for digital reference service and to the exemplary AskA services for setting good examples.

Introduction

Module Profile

This module is intended to welcome readers to *The AskA Starter Kit: How to Build and Maintain Digital Reference Services* (referred to as the Starter Kit) and provide a road map to the resource. At the conclusion of this module, you will be able to achieve the following goal:

Goal
Use the Starter Kit as a guide in building and maintaining a new digital reference, or AskA, service.

Prerequisites
The Starter Kit is intended for organizations interested in offering digital reference service to users in the K–12 community. Such organizations may include libraries, professional associations, government agencies, academic institutions, and companies that specialize in a given subject area or process. This resource is directed towards individuals planning to serve as AskA service administrators or coordinators but could be used as a reference for other staff as well.

Objectives
At the completion of this module, you will be able to achieve the following objectives:
1. Understand the purpose and organizational structure of the Starter Kit.
2. State the six steps in building a digital reference service on which the Starter Kit is based.
3. Understand the goals of the Virtual Reference Desk Project and the benefits of building an AskA Service.

What Is the Starter Kit?

The AskA Starter Kit: How to Build and Maintain Digital Reference Services (also referred to as the Starter Kit) is designed to help organizations build and maintain digital reference services (referred to throughout this document as AskA services). This Starter Kit is intended for organizations that wish to offer human-mediated information services via the Internet to users in the K–12 community. Such organizations include associations, libraries, government agencies, and companies that specialize in a given subject area or skill. While this resource is geared towards service to the K–12 community, the structure and information have wider application in the library and business communities. The information and suggestions made in this document are based on research by the Virtual Reference Desk project (see "What is the Virtual Reference Desk Project?") and input from a panel of representatives from exemplary digital reference services.

The Starter Kit is intended as a set of self-instructional modules for AskA service administrators and other staff. Modules 1 through 6 present the six steps involved in building and maintaining AskA services (see "Starter Kit Structure" below) as self-instructional, interactive modules. Following each module, the reader will achieve a set of goals and objectives as outlined in each module profile. Each module consists of information, examples, and in many cases interactive work sheets for the reader to record important information. Organizations may read the whole Starter Kit from start to finish or concentrate on individual modules as they apply to individual service issues.

Starter Kit Structure

The Starter Kit proposes a six-step process for organizations to follow in creating an AskA service. This process addresses all aspects involved in building and maintaining an AskA service from preliminary research of the digital reference field to ongoing evaluation techniques. Each module of the Starter Kit describes one of the six steps of the overall process and includes statements of goals and objectives for the reader to accomplish; information through explanation and practical examples (e.g., case studies); and opportunities for interaction (e.g., work sheets). The six core modules are outlined below:

1. **Informing:** Collect information on the general digital reference field and existing AskA services.
2. **Planning:** Determine the best way to build and maintain digital reference service within a given organization.
3. **Training:** Plan, produce, implement, and manage training programs for service staff and information specialists.

4. **Prototyping:** Create a prototype and conduct a pilot test of an AskA service.
5. **Contributing:** Manage service development and operations and build partnerships to gain necessary support and share processes.
6. **Evaluating:** Plan and implement evaluation of AskA service and use results to improve service.

Although listed in a linear fashion, the six steps can be completed out of order depending on the needs and experiences of an organization and its AskA service. See Figure 0-1 for a graphical representation of the Starter Kit structure, including goals and objectives of each module.

Module summaries are included at the end of each chapter to highlight key issues for quick reference and review. Wrapping up the Starter Kit is a conclusion, which offers some final notes and a glimpse into the future of digital reference. Other features, including a glossary, case studies, and interactive work sheets, are included for further explanation, illustration, and application of ideas.

Figure 0-1 Six Steps to Building and Maintaining Digital Reference Services

Module	Goals	Objectives
Module 1: Informing	Collect information on the general digital reference field and existing AskA services.	1. Define digital reference, or AskA, services from different perspectives, including library, education, and business. 2. Identify gaps in existing AskA specialization areas. 3. Identify general issues in operating an AskA service. 4. Identify quality characteristics of K–12 digital reference services. 5. Locate information on existing AskA services using the AskA+ Locator. 6. Locate information on potential user population to determine initial need for service.
Module 2: Planning	Determine the best way to build and maintain digital reference service within a given organization.	1. Identify service goals that are consistent with those of supporting organization(s). 2. State components of general structure of AskA services. 3. Create and implement an "AskA plan" for new service. 4. Apply general structure to individual service. 5. Review plans of exemplary AskA services to identify important service components.
Module 3: Training	Plan, produce, implement, and manage training programs for service staff and information specialists.	1. Understand the importance and purpose of planning an effective training program. 2. Identify staff members within the service who require training. 3. State three general phases involved in creating a training program for AskA service staff. 4. Create a plan for an AskA service's training program. 5. Produce the training program by creating materials, preparing delivery tools, and pilot testing materials and activities. 6. Implement the final training program according to planned schedule. 7. Manage the ongoing training program by ongoing evaluation and revision.
Module 4: Prototyping	Create a prototype and conduct a pilot test of an AskA service.	1. Understand the purpose of creating a prototype of an AskA service. 2. Identify common factors in prototypes of AskA services. 3. Describe important components for pilot testing an AskA service prototype. 4. Identify issues and questions to be addressed during a pilot test. 5. Revise prototype based on pilot test results.
Module 5: Contributing	Manage service development and operations and build partnerships to gain necessary support and share processes.	1. Publicize service to potential users. 2. Identify strategies for handling increasing numbers of questions. 3. Create resources to support AskA service. 4. Build partnerships with other organizations to support service. 5. Recruit expert (information specialist) base.
Module 6: Evaluating	Plan and implement evaluation of an AskA service and use results to improve service.	1. Understand the importance and purpose of evaluating an AskA service. 2. Identify areas of the service to be evaluated. 3. Identify standards by which to judge quality of service. 4. Identify methods for obtaining information to evaluate an AskA service. 5. State issues involved in planning an evaluation for an AskA service and apply results.

What Is the Companion Research?

Much of the Starter Kit is based on a year-long study conducted by the Virtual Reference Desk project. This in-depth qualitative study, *Building and Maintaining Internet Information Services: K–12 Digital Reference Services* (Lankes, 1998), is available from the ERIC Clearinghouse on Information & Technology. Many of the pertinent pieces have been either reproduced or simplified for this work. However, the study goes into much more detail on the conceptual foundations of this work and the methods used to create the blueprints presented in Module 2. This study is not essential for the understanding or use of the Starter Kit, but it provides additional detail and support for the scholarly aspects of digital reference work. The Starter Kit complements the research study as a practical guide to creating digital reference services based on the descriptions produced by the study.

What Is the Virtual Reference Desk Project?

The Virtual Reference Desk project is dedicated to creating the foundations for a national cooperative digital reference service. The project is sponsored by the National Library of Education (NLE) and the ERIC Clearinghouse on Information & Technology, with support from the White House Office of Science and Technology Policy.

The Virtual Reference Desk seeks to identify and provide the resources necessary to link all K–12 community members (e.g., students, educators, parents) to necessary expertise in order to satisfy information needs. The goals of the project include research into current ways in which K–12 community members receive answers to questions on the Internet and the development of a national collaborative network of Internet-based question answering services. The Virtual Reference Desk currently provides a Web-based system to help the education community locate existing AskA services and informational and instructional resources to help organizations build new AskA services.

The initial development of the Virtual Reference Desk project included the formation of an expert panel of representatives from existing digital reference services. In sharing their experiences in organizing and managing AskA services, the panel members provided important guidance in creating the Starter Kit.

Module Summary

This section provided an introduction to the *AskA Starter Kit* and the Virtual Reference Desk project.

- The purpose of the Starter Kit is to guide organizations in building and maintaining digital reference, or AskA, services.

- The Starter Kit is organized as a set of self-instructional modules based on a six-step process for creating an AskA service:

    1. Informing
    2. Planning
    3. Training
    4. Prototyping
    5. Contributing
    6. Evaluating

- The Virtual Reference Desk project, sponsored by the National Library of Education and the ERIC Clearinghouse on Information & Technology, is researching current ways in which K–12 community members receive answers to questions on the Internet and is developing a national network of digital reference services.

Module 1

Informing
Planning
Training
Prototyping
Contributing
Evaluating

Informing

Gathering Information on the Current Digital Reference Arena

Module Profile

This module is designed to assist organizations in conducting preliminary research on the digital reference field in preparation for creating new AskA services. At the conclusion of this module, you will be able to achieve the following goal:

Goal   Collect information on the general digital reference field and existing AskA services.

Prerequisites   Before an organization considers providing digital reference service, it must identify its special area of expertise. This area will obviously reflect the focus of the overall organization or special project (see Module 2: Planning). Expertise can take the form of a particular subject area, such as math, physics, or social studies, or a skill area, such as information problem-solving, teaching, or parenting.

Objectives   At the completion of this module, you will be able to achieve the following objectives:

1. Define digital reference, or AskA, services from different perspectives, including library, education, and business.
2. Identify gaps in existing AskA specialization areas.
3. Identify general issues in operating an AskA service.
4. Identify quality characteristics of K–12 digital reference services.
5. Locate information on existing AskA services using the AskA+ Locator.
6. Locate information on the potential user population to determine initial need for service.

7

1.1 Introduction to Digital Reference and AskA Services

What Are Digital Reference and AskA Services?

Digital reference services are Internet-based question-and-answer services that connect users with individuals who possess specialized subject or skill expertise. As opposed to static Web pages, digital reference services use the Internet to place people in contact with those individuals who can answer specific questions and instruct users in developing certain skills. Digital reference services are also referred to as AskA services, because of such service names as Ask A Volcanologist, Ask A Scientist, etc.

Hundreds of digital reference services exist today, many of them serving the K–12 community. Some examples include

- AskERIC, a project of the Educational Resources Information Center (ERIC) since 1992, which places teachers, librarians, parents, and others in contact with information specialists who provide pointers to education information sources (Lankes, 1995).

- KidsConnect, a project of the American Association of School Librarians, which places K–12 students in contact with school library media specialists who help them find Internet and non-Internet resources to answer their questions (Bennett, 1997).

- Ask Dr. Math from the Math Forum at Swarthmore College, a team of mathematicians (or "math doctors") who respond to K–12 students' questions about math *http://forum.swarthmore.edu/dr.math/*

- Ask A Scientist from the MAD Scientist Network (of the Medical School at Washington University in St. Louis), which allows students to ask questions of science experts *http://www.madsci.org*

While many AskA services cater to K–12 audiences on topics relating to curriculum areas, digital reference services also represent other contexts, including library and business. The context of digital reference (in addition to other factors) often dictates the overall goals, day-to-day operations, and scope of the service. Digital reference has its roots in the library field but affects and draws from experiences of education and business contexts.

Digital Reference From an Education Perspective

The Internet can be an effective and motivational learning tool when used in context with educational goals and objectives. It adds an interactive dimension to K–12 education by enabling students, educators, parents, and others to communicate with each other and with subject and skill experts all over the world. Students can learn firsthand about life in Antarctica by corresponding with a meteorologist who regularly visits the continent (*http://www.theice.org/*). Library media specialists can discuss lesson-planning ideas with colleagues on a 7,000+-member e-mail discussion group called LM_NET (*http://ericir.syr.edu/lm_net/*). Parents can receive advice on helping children with study skills by contacting educational researchers at Parents AskERIC from the National Parent Information Network (*http://ericps.ed.uiuc.edu/npin/*).

Digital reference services maximize this interactive nature of the Internet by providing expertise in response to questions as well as direction in enabling users to answer their questions independently. AskA services normally respond to individual queries on a one-time basis; this differs from mentoring programs, which connect students and teachers to subject-matter experts for longer term curriculum-based projects (for example, see Sanchez & Harris, 1996).

However, most exemplary digital reference services agree that it is not enough for experts or information specialists to simply offer *answers*. Digital reference services can prepare users in the K–12 community—students, teachers, parents, etc.—to become effective information problem solvers. In other words, digital reference services can play a significant role in helping people develop skills for critical thinking and assessment of information resources to apply to any context at any stage of life.[1]

---

[1] For more information on how digital reference services can carry out their instructional role through responses, see Kasowitz (1998).

Digital Reference from a Library Perspective

Libraries are becoming an increasingly visible presence on the Internet, with many launching Web sites and offering digital pathfinders to other online resources and collections. As with many organizations that have established an Internet presence, libraries are currently exploring ways in which to expand their services by interacting with users and responding to inquiries via the Internet. For libraries, this type of virtual interaction is an extension of the face-to-face or telephone reference service already offered. Digital reference, sometimes referred to as electronic reference in the library field, allows library users to access a human intermediary at their own convenience without having to physically enter the library facility.

Libraries as AskA Services

Libraries, like subject-oriented AskA services, engage in digital reference by directing users to appropriate online or print resources and/or providing factual information. Occasionally user queries must be clarified, and an online reference interview may be conducted to help define the user's information needs. Examples of library-based digital reference services are seen mostly in academic and public libraries.

While many academic libraries have established digital reference services, most restrict their services to their local academic communities only. Common methods of limiting access to services include password protection or Internet Protocol (IP) address mapping. Some academic libraries, such as Roger Williams University Library in Bristol, Rhode Island[2], currently accept questions from the general public, but these libraries tend to have modest question loads at the present time.

Public libraries, though slower to implement digital reference services than academic libraries, typically accept questions from the general population. Some libraries such as the Seattle Public Library (SPL) restrict their services to valid SPL cardholders only, while others do not publicize their services in order to limit the number of questions received.

The following pages discuss digital reference in a library context in terms of the impacts of the Internet reference service, changing roles of reference librarians, and digital libraries. This discussion is included as an excerpt from the companion research report *Building and Maintaining Internet Information Services: K-12 Digital Reference Services* available from ERIC Clearinghouse on Information and Technology (Lankes, 1998).

---

[2] Information from personal communication, Susan McMullen, Information Resources Librarian at Roger Williams University Library November 14, 1998.

Defining Digital Reference Services

For the purposes of this study, reference services are defined as mediated interfaces between users in an "anomalous state of knowledge" (Belkin, 1980) and a collection of information (Sutton, 1996, p.131-3). The user's anomalous state of knowledge, also referred to as a gap in cognitive understanding (Dervin & Nilan, 1986), is operationalized in this study as a question that needs to be answered. This question may be expressed as an e-mail request or a query to a system (Taylor, 1968). The collection is a set of information in the form of documents, files and/or knowledge (including human expertise). In this study, all information was delivered to a user electronically via the Internet[3]

Mediation between the user and the query is the central topic of reference research. Mediation can be performed either through a human expert (such as a reference librarian) or an automated interface (such as an online catalog). The primary purpose of the interface is to match the user's information need to the system's organization and capabilities (Taylor, 1968). The mediator (once again, either automated or human) becomes the user's advocate to the system or collection. This view of reference is maintained in today's electronic reference environment (Sutton, 1996). This study concentrated on how organizations, specifically K-12 digital reference services, built Internet information systems that fulfilled users' reference needs. Restating the concentration of this study using language from the reference discussion above: how organizations built and maintained information services that mediated between a user's information need and a collection of information.

Impacts of the Internet on Reference Services

The literature shows significant impacts on reference services prompted by greater access to the Internet and Internet tools. These impacts include new skills needed by information specialists and reference librarians (Bobp, Kratzert & Richey, 1993). The Internet is also expanding traditional library collections and improving location and access[4] to reference resources (i.e, ready reference materials and pathfinders through World Wide Web sites, access to catalogs and electronic reference sources through telnet, etc). Most significant to this research, the Internet affords reference services the ability to conduct entire reference transactions (from specifying users' needs to delivering information from the collection) via the Internet (Still & Campbell, 1993).

A great deal of literature has focused on augmenting traditional reference services with Internet resources and capabilities. This literature ranges from evaluation criteria for on-line reference sources (Balas, 1995) to discussions of technology used to locate and access Internet resources (examples include Feeney, 1993; Bobp, Katzert & Richey, 1993; Gainor & Foster, 1993; Arms, 1990; Branse, 1993; Machovec, 1993). In these discussions, the interface to the user remains the same, but the collection is expanded to include Internet resources. These new resources change the reference environment. Mardikian and Kesselman (1995, p. 22-3) presented five "rationales for changing reference:"

---

[3]This can be done through client/server systems like the World Wide Web or other systems such as e-mail.
[4]For a discussion on location and access see Eisenberg and Berkowitz, 1990, p.7.

- Increasing access to resources beyond the library (networked resources including the Internet).
- Lack of geographic constraints for users ("users may no longer need to come to the library to obtain information").
- The need to differentiate services to different populations of users (i.e., inside an organization and outside an organization) in the face of shrinking budgets.
- Increases in complexity of information resources and the need for specialized knowledge.
- New options (primarily in staffing) for answering reference questions.

All of these rationales concentrate on having librarians redefine their roles within a traditional, geographically defined library setting.

Changing Roles of Reference Librarians

These changes in the reference environment focus on the reference librarian and the training of that librarian in response to the "increasingly automated [library] over the past three decades" (He & Knee, 1995 p.7). He and Knee presented the idea of an electronic services librarian. In regards to reference services, they stated, "It is important for electronic services librarians to be familiar with traditional as well as electronic reference sources. By learning traditional sources, they will be able to recognize which Internet resources may also be valuable" (p. 9). He and Knee called for librarians to update their skills in response to perceived changes to the reference environment. Librarians' skills must also include an ability to evaluate networked resources. McClure (1994) discussed the evaluation of networked resources. He drew upon VanHouse et al. (1990) to define evaluation as "the process of identifying and collecting data about specific services or activities, establishing criteria by which their success can be assessed, and determining both the quality of the service or activity and the degree to which the service or activity accomplishes stated goals and objectives" (McClure 1994, p.592).

The burden of learning and applying the application and evaluation skills of the Internet falls upon the librarian. The librarian must master the new Internet tools for his or her users. The reference librarian acts as "a bridge which has technology at one end and the user at the other" (Callahan, 1991). Learning, however, is not limited to just applications and technology. It also applies to learning to deal with change. McClure et al. stated "library staff . . . must learn from their colleagues in the computing services how to become more comfortable with the type and rate of change that will accompany the networked environment" (McClure, Moen & Ryan, 1994). This notion of change and the need for technical proficiency is echoed throughout most of the literature concerning reference services and the Internet. The use of complexity in this research was a reaction to the fact that digital reference services must also deal with a great amount of change.

Accompanying the changes in reference librarians' skills are changes in the reference librarians' roles, particularly in regards to staffing. Oberg states "paraprofessionals can and do perform well at a reference desk, freeing librarians to concentrate on higher-level tasks" (from Mardikian & Kesselman, 1995, p.21). Mardikian and Kesselman presented a three level staffing model to reflect the changing role of the reference librarian (see Table 2-1).

Table 2-1: Mardikian and Kesselman's Staffing Levels (From *Building and Maintaining Internet Information Services: K-12 Digital Reference Services*)

Level 1: Minimum Human Intervention
• Self-guided building tours • Automated telephone answering machines • Better signage • Better floor maps • Library quick guides • Step-by-step guides • Computer-assisted instruction for self-service instruction • Computerized information kiosks
Level 2: Library Interns/Trained Paraprofessional Staff
• General library orientation and general bibliographic instruction • Directional inquiries • Ready reference searching • Bibliographic verification on OCLC, RLIN, and the online catalog • Assist with search strategy formulation • Technical assistance with machine problems • Basic informational services with referrals as needed
Level 3: Librarians, Subject Specialists
• Individual research consultations • Specialized reference services • Office hours in departments • Member of a research team with teaching faculty • Liaison activities with departments • Specialized instructional services • Integrate information literacy into the curriculum • Research and development efforts • Mediated online searching • Create CAI programs and expert systems for users • Ongoing evaluation and needs assessment

From this table the researcher assumed that most information specialists working in K-12 digital reference services would fall into category three with some in category two.

Accompanying this shift in responsibilities for reference librarians (to higher-level tasks) is a call for greater collaboration with other types of professionals. Lewis (1995) believed the infusion of new tools for location and access into libraries means "a significant upgrading of skills of most librarians and will mean professionals who are not librarians will have to be offered positions along side of, or in place of, librarians." McClure, et al. (1994, p.67) listed partnering with computing services, faculty, and other "external organizations and companies" as critical success factors in building the virtual library. One would expect members of digital reference services to be highly knowledgeable in technology and Internet applications. However, as discussed in Chapter 4, few services have specific detectors for infrastructure issues such as hardware and wiring, instead relying on their larger organizations for such knowledge. Indeed, these services have formed strong relationships with computing centers and technical organizations as discussed by McClure et al. (1994).

The literature did, however, allow the researcher to anticipate that information specialists in K-12 digital reference services would have backgrounds other than library and information science. Indeed while the two pretest services of this study (AskERIC and the Internet Public Library) claimed strong backgrounds in formal library training, only one of the six services studied (The National Museum of American Art Reference Desk) employed a professional librarian.

Digital Libraries

The Internet is also used to provide better access to a library's collection. The Internet is used to organize materials for reference patrons[22] (Jensen & Sih, 1995) and allow patrons access to reference sources such as OPACs[6] (He & Knee, 1995). This reference collection literature includes discussions of standards for information interchange (Moen, 1992). The literature seems to present a continuum for reference services and access in relation to the Internet. There has been a general belief that libraries and reference services are headed "towards a virtual future" (Strong, 1996). However, this future has not been widely explored.

Sutton's (1996) four-part typology of libraries anticipated the expansion of reference collections to include the Internet, as well as the use of the Internet to access an individual library's collection. This four part typology (see Figure 2-1) created a continuum from a paper-based ("traditional") library to a fully "digital" library without walls (Sutton, 1996, p.129). It consists of:

- Traditional: "a specific place with a finite collection of tangible information bearing primary entities like books and journals . . . [denoted as] paper" (Sutton, 1996, p. 131).
- Automated: a mix of paper and digital reference resources and meta-information that "point to non-digital media" (Sutton, 1996, p. 135).
- Hybrid: typified by the use of both print and digital meta-information sources (increasingly digital) and the coexistence of both digital and paper primary resources. This type of library allows for the first time remote access to "some subset of the library's digital collection or to digital resources"(Sutton, 1996, p. 136).
- Digital: ". . . the library as a logical entity. It is the library without walls—the library does not collect tangible information bearing entities but instead provides mediated, geographically unconstrained access to distributed, networked digital information" (Sutton, 1996, p. 138).

From this typology, Internet information systems, specifically digital reference services, can be seen as "digital" libraries. Since such services transact all information delivery via the Internet, they are fully digital.

One interesting aspect of a digital library's reference services is the ability of the Internet to hide the process of reference services. Still and Campbell noted:

> . . . one big difference [between traditional reference interactions and using the Internet for reference work] was that e-mail has made the internal operations of the library invisible to the patron; they are unaware of which department handles each request. The patron simply asks the question" (1993 p. 16).

---

[5]Patron is a library term synonymous with user or customer.
[6]An OPAC is an Online Public Access Catalog. It is a computer database that allows library patrons access to information on a library's collection.

The present study was a direct response to the "black box" effect[7] of the Internet. K-12 digital reference services are being built and used, but it is impossible to determine more than the most rudimentary processes within the actual reference process.[8] Most services in their public documentation and description concentrate on what the service does, not how it is done.

Sutton (1996) stated that in a digital library the primary task of the librarian is to provide "context" (Sutton refers to Saffo's [1994] concept of context). That is to say, the collection becomes so large (it could be considered to consist of the entire Internet) that patrons no longer desire the full range of information available on a given topic, but the "best" information. The librarian's role shifts from advocate to a collection to a filter for the user. Since the patron is no longer bound by geography (or technology), the user will select services based on how well they create a context useful to that user. So the selection of K-12 digital reference services could be seen as a selection of contexts.

Digital Reference Services Summary

Reference librarianship and reference services have a long and rich history. It is clear from the literature that the Internet has a major impact on how reference services are accomplished in the networked world. A continuum appears to have been established (see Figure 2-1). The continuum starts at a library with no automation, unaware of the Internet, and ends in a library as "logical entity" (Sutton, 1996, p. 131) where reference services provide context to a globally distributed, fully digital collection. Much of the discussions within this literature centers on the role of the reference librarian. The librarian or information specialist of the fully digital library appears to be technically literate, but versed in traditional reference resources; cooperative with organizations outside of the library; prepared to cope with great change; and able to provide context to patrons. These characteristics certainly apply to the services studied in this research, even though they do not have formal library training.

---

[7]A black box effect is used to refer to a system where only the input and output are known. However, one is unable to determine the means that transform input into output.
[8]Some services make such information explicit. For example, the AskERIC service not only includes information on who is answering a question, but also on the way in which that question was answered.

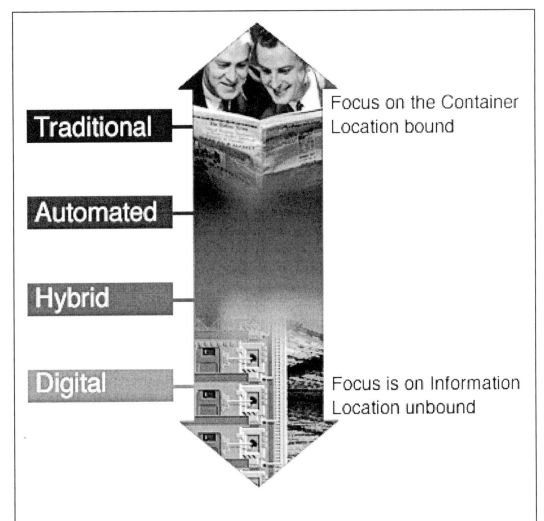

Figure 2-1 Continuum of Libraries: Sutton (1996) establishes a continuum of libraries from "traditional" that is bound by its physical facilities and concentrates on "objects" such as books to "digital" in which the network and electronic documents make objects and location irrelevant. (From *Building and Maintaining Internet Information Services: K-12 Digital Reference Services.*)

This literature informed the researcher as to the importance of this study (to counteract the black box effect created by Internet digital reference services) and built a set of anticipated characteristics of information professionals within these digital reference services. This literature led the researcher to expect information specialists would be technically literate and from a wide variety of backgrounds. The expertise on the part of digital reference service workers was accounted for in the methodology. However, the researcher could also expect the builders and maintainers of these services to be able to understand and explain both the processes of their Internet information services and the technology resources used. This combination (process knowledge and technical knowledge) supported the choice of K-12 digital reference services as the population for this study. The following sections build a conceptual framework used to explore the "digital library" environment facilitated by the Internet.

Digital Reference From a Business Perspective

Business has long understood the importance of a human-to-human connection with users, whether the users be business partners, customers, or employees. Recent articles have highlighted the importance of call centers and help desks in companies (see Bibliography —Business).

Help desks normally utilize special software to track internal software or product problems. These systems assign "ticket number" or "incident" reports to staff problems, catalog system personnel and their specialties, and store and track answers as they are created. In these systems, a knowledge base is created over the life of the system consisting of problems encountered over time. The staff at the help desk tend to be specialists or experts. The goal of the system is to track problems and make sure they are answered in a timely manner, while capturing novel solutions for future reuse.

Call centers operate differently from help desks. These systems tend to be telephone-based and support known answers. In these systems a set of known answers exist in a knowledge base, and a series of scripts leads a relatively inexperienced customer service representative through a predetermined set of steps to determine a set course of action. The classic example is the "broken toaster" scenario in which a customer with a broken toaster calls a service line. The call is routed to the next available representative. Upon making a connection with the customer, a representative launches into a series of scripted questions meant to narrow possible known solutions (e.g., "Is it plugged in?" "Do the heating elements turn red?" "Do you smell smoke?"). These systems work in areas with a finite set of answers, where the process is to get to a known solution. If a known solution does not exist, the customer is normally taken out of this system and transferred to another system, such as an engineer, or the item is returned so that another department can take a look at it.

Both of these types of solutions belong to a larger class of software known as work-flow solutions. These solutions involve a large analysis component followed by a stratification of a business process into a series of layers. These layers classically consist of

- process logic: the business rules and established procedures for acting upon information
- information resources: data, hardware, and software applications that manage and manipulate data
- human resources: experts, managers, and other organizational employees (Stark, 1997).

These layers are put in place so that an organization can effectively process information or an event (say a request for information) effectively. By stratifying these layers, components at each layer can be replaced without disrupting the other layer.

Work-flow solutions are embracing the Web and Internet. While there have been some delays and turbulence as they grapple with a new business environment (for example, changing from a costing based on "number of customer service seats" to simultaneous connections), these software vendors are beginning to use the Web to provide common interfaces. However, there has been little attempt to create methods of exchange among these packages.

Summary of Digital Reference From Multiple Perspectives

Building from experiences of libraries, education, and business, organizations have already begun to build and operate AskA services. Together, these AskA services represent a new, distinct field with common issues, characteristics, and quality standards.

1.2 Current Trends and Issues in AskA Services

The digital reference field is diverse and dynamic. Existing services range from one- or two-person "Mom and Pop" operations to services staffed by over 400 "expert" employees or volunteers. Numbers of questions answered range from two to over 200 per day (see AskA Capacity Matrix *http://www.vrd.org/AskA/capacity.htm*). Despite the differences among AskA services in size, scope, etc., AskA services do share some common issues. This section describes the state of AskA services today in terms of expertise areas as well as common issues regarding operations and service quality. This information is provided to help organizations prepare to start planning their own services. It attempts to answer these questions: What's out there? What should new services expect?

Survey of AskA Services' Specialty Areas

AskA services provide information in a variety of subject and skill specialties (e.g., health, science, math, etc.). As in any type of business or service industry, it is helpful to engage in some market research before providing a new AskA service. An organization should review the arena of existing services before offering a new service in a certain specialization area. Depending on current representation of a particular topic, an organization may choose to focus specifically on a subspecialty (e.g., geography of Canada) or to broaden the scope of the service (e.g., geography).

With hundreds of new Web sites appearing daily, the Internet can be a rich source of information for students, parents, and educators. Increasing numbers of universities, organizations, and other entities are offering AskA services to the K–12 community. However, despite the proliferation of AskA services, many subject areas remain inadequately represented with few or no services in effect. For example, while users seeking information from scientists or reference librarians have several services from which to choose, those seeking interaction with art and art education experts find very few services available (e.g., see "A Report of Art and Art Education AskA Services" at the end of this module). Other subject areas such as history, literature, foreign language, and world geography are similarly underrepresented. To further enhance and support K–12 teaching and learning efforts, all subject areas should be represented for comprehensive coverage.

At the present time, for example, there are no AskA services answering questions on the American Civil War, or European or Asian art for the general public. The addition of such services, and their personal replies to student inquiries, can capture students' interest and further motivate them to explore such subject areas more fully on their own. Due to the lack of digital reference services in subject areas such as art, history, and others, however, the information needs of many users may be left unmet. Moreover, a potential burden may be placed on the few services that do exist in underrepresented subject areas, as the question volume may prove to be overwhelming for too few services to effectively manage.

The AskA Overviews located at the end of this module provide surveys of AskA services in two distinct subject areas: art and paleontology. They offer summaries of existing AskA services in specific subject areas in order to help organizations plan for the development of similar yet distinct AskA services.

Issues in AskA Services

Although digital reference services can vary in many aspects including number of staff, number of questions answered, technology used, and subject areas covered, they do experience many common issues. All AskA services grapple with issues of policy, operation, and management. For instance, many services are familiar with the experience of starting what they had planned to be a small, controlled question-answer service for a specific population (possibly as an outgrowth of another Web resource or initiative) only to very quickly become overwhelmed by hundreds of questions from the general Internet public. In addition, many services struggle with legal issues regarding liability for information provided and confidentiality of user information posted on services' Web sites. Common issues are summarized on the following pages.

Legal and Ethical Issues

User Confidentiality. AskA services that plan to make user correspondence public through a question-answer archive, etc., should consider how they will ensure confidentiality of any information that can be used to identify a user (e.g., name, e-mail address, postal address, phone number, etc.). This is especially important when dealing with K–12 students since educators and parents may discourage children from providing personal information that will be accessible to all Internet users worldwide. This concept is consistent with the American Library Association's Policy on Confidentiality of Library Records (American Library Association, 1986) and the American Library Association Code of Ethics, which states "We protect each library user's right to privacy and confidentiality with respect to information sought or received and resources consulted, borrowed, acquired or transmitted" (American Library Association, 1995 Online). It is only appropriate that AskA services adopt core policies and philosophies of established library associations. (See Module 5: Contributing, for suggestions on ensuring user confidentiality.)

Service Liability. Services rely on their information specialists to provide information based on expertise and knowledge. Services should make sure that users are aware of the limits on information provided. This is especially important for services whose expert information can be interpreted as professional advice (e.g., medical, legal, etc.) but is a valid concern for all types of digital reference services. For example, an AskA service providing information on dental care should be clear in stating that the dental expert's response is not a substitute for a consultation with the user's dentist. Similarly, library-based electronic reference services should make the same type of statement when referring users to dental information and especially when including any information taken from related information resources. (See Module 5: Contributing, for suggestions and examples regarding service liability.)

Copyright. While AskA service information specialists normally provide original expert information or referrals to information resources, there are times when they include information taken from other sources. In writing an AskA service response, information specialists should give credit to appropriate sources the way they would when writing other types of documents. While this issue is always important in providing information, it is especially crucial for services that provide public access to question-answer collections.

Services may also be concerned with copyrighting information on their own site (e.g., question-answer archive, information resources, etc.). While this is not an option for many services (especially those with government sponsorship), other services can rely on their parent organizations' copyright policies if available. (See Module 5: Contributing, for suggestions on handling copyright issues.)

Operational Issues

Lack of Software. Currently, there is a lack of software available to assist AskA services in managing the question-answer process. Some services have attempted to automate the question-answer process by developing original software packages (many based on PERL scripts). Examples of PERL-based software work-flow packages are *MODERATOR* from the MAD Scientist Network (Bry, 1997) and the *Doctor's Office* from Ask Dr. Math (The Math Forum, 1998). Other services manage the process using an e-mail program and a pencil and paper to record question routing activities.[9]

Staff Recruitment and Management. An AskA service can require anywhere from one to 500+ staff members. Various job roles include service administrator-coordinator (managing day-to-day operations and long-term decision making), experts (responding to user questions; often volunteers), support staff (overseeing the work of experts; sometimes called moderators, team leaders, etc.), and technical staff (developing Web resources, software, etc.). These staff roles are not always distinct; often one or two people will overlap several roles. However, these roles do represent the main functions involved in maintaining an AskA service. Issues relating to AskA service staff include recruiting, training, and quality control.

Funding. Most AskA services operate on a not-for-profit basis, meaning that they must acquire funding from an external (or internal) source. Common sources include the government, professional organizations, universities, and corporations. In some cases, a service is an added function of a larger existing organization (e.g., Ask Shamu from Sea World/Busch Gardens). In many cases, services must actively seek funding through grant-writing activities. See Wasik (1998) for suggestions and resources to help services seek funding.

Marketing and Publicity. While some services openly embrace the opportunity to attract users, others are more hesitant for fear that they may receive more questions than they can handle. Different techniques for advertising a service include registering the service with a Web search engine, placing notices on other organizations' Web sites, and posting messages on related electronic discussion groups, etc. (See Module 5: Contributing, for more suggestions and examples).

---

[9] Remedy Corporation is working with the Virtual Reference Desk to develop a customizable software package to help individual AskA services manage their question-answer and archiving processes.

Question-Answer Policy. Answering user questions is not always as straightforward as it may sound. Decisions must be made early on regarding the following questions: What types of questions will and will not be answered? What are the necessary components to include in a response? How will vague user queries be handled? What is the turnaround time for a response? Decisions on these issues will aid staff in conducting day-to-day tasks and will help services focus on intended goals. (See Module 2: Planning, for further discussion on question-answer policy.)

Supplemental Resources. Most services offer some type of Web-based resource to supplement their question-answer service; in some cases, it is the service that supplements the pre-existing resources. The most popular types of resources are question-answer archives[10] and collections of frequently asked questions, or FAQs. Other resources may include supplemental information about a popular topic and lists of links to other resources. Services often encourage users to review the collections first before submitting an original question. Issues related to supplemental resources include type of user interface, number of question-answer sets included, frequency with which resources are updated, and staff member(s) responsible for resource maintenance.

Dealing with AskA Service Issues

Later modules of this Starter Kit will discuss many of these issues as noted, although there are no hard and fast rules for ensuring that these issues are resolved smoothly. Case studies are included to illustrate ways that existing services have dealt with various issues in their experiences.

Quality Characteristics and Standards

Besides some common issues and trends, certain characteristics have been identified to determine the quality of an AskA service for the K–12 community. The Virtual Reference Desk Expert Panel identified 12 characteristics and features (referred to as "facets of quality") for building a digital reference service for the K–12 educational community. The facets of quality are based upon panel members' experiences in managing and coordinating exemplary digital reference services. This list is intended as a set of standards for organizations to achieve in creating and maintaining digital reference services in ways that accommodate specific service requirements and characteristics.

---

[10] The Virtual Reference Desk is developing a knowledge base of question-answer sets from a consortium of services to enable users to search from a comprehensive collection of questions and answers before sending a question to a particular service.

The facets are divided into two main categories: user transaction and service development/management. The user transaction category includes those components that occur during the question-answer process; these features are generally visible to the user. The service development/management category involves decisions made in creating and maintaining the service that affect overall quality and user satisfaction.

The 12 "facets of quality" are listed below (see the following pages for a complete discussion):

User Transaction
1. Accessible
2. Prompt turnaround
3. Sets user expectations
4. Interactive
5. Instructive

Service Development and Management
6. Authoritative
7. Trained information specialists
8. Private
9. Reviewed
10. Unbiased
11. Provides access to related information
12. Publicized

Facets of Quality for K-12 Digital Reference Services

The Virtual Reference Desk Expert Panel has identified twelve characteristics and features (referred to as facets of quality) for building a digital reference service for the K–12 educational community. The facets of quality are based upon panel members' experiences in managing and coordinating exemplary digital reference services. This list is intended as a set of standards for organizations to achieve in creating and maintaining digital reference services.

The facets are divided into two main categories: user transaction and service development and management. The user transaction category includes those components that occur during the question-answer process; these features are generally visible to the user. The service development and management category involves decisions made in creating and maintaining the service that affect overall quality and user satisfaction.

It is important to note that K–12 digital reference services differ from each other in several aspects including policy and procedure, subject matter expertise, and supporting technology. Each service should apply the recommendations below in ways that accommodate its specific requirements and characteristics.

User Transaction

ACCESSIBLE

Definition. K–12 digital reference services should be easily reachable and navigable by any Internet user regardless of equipment sophistication. (Many users connect from school-based computer systems that may not have high bandwidth capabilities.)

Strategies. Digital reference services can maximize accessibility by:
- Providing options for contacting the service (i.e., offer e-mail address and Web form)
- Designing a Web interface that accommodates users with low-bandwidth capabilities (i.e., minimal graphics and animation).

PROMPT TURNAROUND

Definition. All questions should be addressed as quickly as possible. Actual turnaround time depends on a service's question-answer policy and available resources (e.g., staffing, funds, etc.).

Strategies. Some exemplary digital reference services strive to answer inquiries within two business days, while others plan to take longer (e.g., up to two weeks).

SETS USER EXPECTATIONS

Definition. Clear communication should occur either before or at the start of every digital reference transaction in order to reduce opportunities for user confusion and inappropriate inquiries.

Strategies. Question-answer procedures and services should be stated clearly either on a Web site or in an automated request acknowledgment to the user. Statements should include the following items:

- Time frame for returning response
- Format of response (e.g., what it will include, where response will appear)
- Rate of questions answered by service
- Expert qualifications of:
  - ◊ Service
  - ◊ Those providing answers (information specialists)
  - ◊ Resources consulted to find answers.

INTERACTIVE

Definition. Digital reference services should provide opportunities for users to communicate necessary information to information specialists and to clarify vague user questions. The more opportunities for interaction, the more effective the transaction.

Strategies. Important information—such as user age or grade level, other sources checked, contact information—can be captured through the following mechanisms:
- Web-based request form
- Interactive communication tools (e.g., chat room).

In addition, user questions can be clarified through follow-up e-mail messages or conversations using interactive communications tools.

INSTRUCTIVE

Definition. Digital reference services can play an important role in the learning processes of both children and adults by providing access to current information and expertise. Quality digital reference services offer more to users than straight, factual answers; they guide them in subject knowledge as well as the area of information literacy.

Strategies. Information specialists can offer pointers and paths used to find the best resources, so users can learn to answer similar questions on their own. For example, information specialists can mention the tools used to find resources (e.g., search engines, indexes, bibliographies, catalogs), specific search terms and processes used, and series of steps taken.

Service Development and Management

AUTHORITATIVE

Definition. The information specialists of a digital reference service should have the necessary knowledge and educational background in the service's given subject area or skill in order to qualify as an expert.

Strategies. Specific levels of knowledge, skill and experience are determined by each service and its related discipline or field.

TRAINED INFORMATION SPECIALISTS

Definition. Services should offer effective orientation or training processes to prepare information specialists to respond to inquiries using clear and effective language and following service response guidelines. Training of information specialists is one of the most important aspects of planning and operating a digital reference service.

Strategies. Many possible training models exist for digital reference services. Training components include written documents containing response guidelines and opportunities for information specialists to practice responding to inquiries accompanied by feedback on performance. (See Kasowitz [1998] for background and information on general skills involved in composing responses for the K-12 community.)

PRIVATE

Definition. All communications between users and information specialists should be held in complete privacy.

Strategies. Digital reference services should receive consent from users before sharing transaction data or identification information (e.g., e-mail address) with a third party (e.g., questions and answers posted in a Web-based archive).

REVIEWED

Definition. Digital reference services should regularly evaluate their processes and services (i.e., responses). Ongoing review and assessment helps ensure quality, efficiency, and reliability of transactions as well as overall user satisfaction.

Strategies. Evaluation mechanisms can include review of information specialists' responses, survey of users and feedback from information specialists.

UNBIASED

Definition. Digital reference services should not promote products or personal and institutional opinions in such a way that interferes with quality or use of service. This is especially important because adults in the K–12 community (e.g., parents, administrators, teachers) may be concerned with children's access to Internet-based information.

Strategies. Some ways to avoid bias in service responses and materials include the following:
- Provide a balanced set of resources and provide statements of context for any type of opinion or viewpoint (e.g., "research states . . .," "some people believe . . .," etc.).
- When including information from another source, include full bibliographic citations to emphasize that the information provided is not expressing a personal opinion.
- If commercial advertisements must be included, they should not interfere with the primary information provided by the service (e.g., place product logos as smaller icons at the bottom of a Web page).

PROVIDES ACCESS TO RELATED INFORMATION

Definition. Besides offering direct response to user questions, digital reference services should offer access to supporting resources and information.

Strategies. This can include information on a service's special content area, access to a knowledge base of previously-asked questions and answers, and links or references to external resources. Web sites should be reviewed and updated regularly to ensure that content is correct and links and references are active.

PUBLICIZED

Definition. Services providing information to the K–12 community are responsible for informing potential users of the value that can be gained from use of the service. The greater the outreach to K-12 communities across the country, the smaller the gap between the "haves" and the "have-nots" in terms of effective learning opportunities.

Strategies: A well-defined public relations plan can ensure that services are well-publicized and promoted on a regular basis. Methods for publicizing a digital reference service may include:
- Direct mail campaigns to potential users
- Promotional messages to appropriate electronic discussion groups (e.g., listservs)
- References to the service on related Web sites (in the form of information as well as links)
- A Web site of resources that points users to the question/answer service as well as supporting information resources.

Conclusion

K–12 digital reference services play an important role in leading students, parents, teachers, and others to information on and off the Internet. New and existing digital reference services can carry out this educational role by using the above recommendations as a guide in service decisions and question-answer transactions.

From *http://www.vrd.org/training/facets.html*. Compiled by Abby Kasowitz. Content is based on discussion of Virtual Reference Desk Expert Panel members (July to December 1997) moderated by David Lankes. Original panel members included Blythe Bennett of KidsConnect, Lynn Bry of the MAD Scientist Network, Martha Dexter of the Library of Congress, Peter Milbury of LM_NET, Joan Stahl of the National Museum of American Art/Smithsonian, Robin Summers of AskERIC, Steve Weimar of the Math Forum, and Ken Williams of the Math Forum.

1.3 Tools and Methods for Gathering AskA and Audience Information

An organization can use information about general trends in the digital reference field and common issues and characteristics to begin exploring the environment in context of one's own plans for digital reference service. This section discusses tools for researching existing services and methods for exploring potential user needs. This type of research can help organizations decide whether or not to provide service or to focus on a specific area in terms of content or nature of service.

Gathering Information About AskA Services: The AskA+ Locator

Organizations can research existing AskA services on their own to find information relevant to their interests and intended direction of a potential service. One way to conduct this type of research is by searching the Virtual Reference Desk's AskA+ Locator, a Web based collection of high-quality AskA services that focus on the information needs of the K–12 community. The AskA+ Locator can be found at *http://www.vrd.org/locator/index.html*

The Locator was initially developed in the summer of 1997 as an information resource for both K–12 users seeking answers to questions and for AskA services requiring question answering support and resource referral.

Potential services were culled from a variety of sources, including resource lists such as Pitsco's Ask an Expert site *http://www.askanexpert.com/askanexpert/*, federal agencies such as NASA, and other educational sites and organizations. Additional AskA services were located through the use of Internet search engines by using a variety of keyword searches.

Each site was reviewed for its target audience (educators, students, parents), the subject area, its applicability to curricular needs, and other criteria as set forth by the Virtual Reference Desk Expert Panel (see "Facets of Quality"). In some instances, interviews were conducted with services to elicit more information regarding the nature of the service and its operations.

The Locator is a dynamic resource; defunct services are removed and new services are added as they become available. An online submission form at *http://www.vrd.org/locator/form.html* is available at the Virtual Reference Desk Web site so that AskA services can submit their information and URL(s) for possible inclusion in the Locator. Each submission is then reviewed and evaluated to ensure that certain standards of quality are met. The Locator also lists only those AskA services that are free to the general public: Although there are several quality fee-based services available, the Virtual Reference Desk lists only those services that offer equal access to all users regardless of economic status.

The Locator differs from other Web-based collections of AskA services in a few key areas:

- The Locator includes only those services that serve the K–12 community and meet some minimal quality criteria as identified by the Virtual Reference Desk Expert Panel.

- Detailed meta-descriptions are provided for each service in the Locator. These "Profiles" include service identification information (e.g., e-mail address, contact person, links to services' home pages), scope, target audience, and a general description. Each profile links directly to the AskA service's home page and question submission page.

- A search engine is built in to allow users from the K–12 community as well as those researching AskA services to locate services by keyword.

- Besides offering a search engine, the Locator provides subject and alphabetical listings of all services included.

Some organizations may use the AskA+ Locator to find services in a particular subject area. For instance an organization interested in providing an astronomy AskA service may want to survey the field of existing AskAs to see if there's an aspect of astronomy that is not currently met by existing astronomy services. Such an organization could use the Locator in this way:

> Go directly to the subject listing, *http://www.vrd.org/locator/subject.html*, and scroll down to the heading "Science," subheading "Astronomy." Here one will find a list of 10 services that already address questions dealing with astronomy. To learn about each service in more detail, one can click on the title of each service and go directly to its profile. The profile will reveal such information as
> - question- "answerers" (e.g., astronomers, astronauts, classroom teachers, etc.)
> - scope of subject areas addressed (e.g., space sciences, science careers, general science, etc.)
> - service operation (e.g., answers all questions vs. representative sample, includes archive of previously asked questions, etc.).

Using this type of information, organizations can determine whether or not (or to what extent) they can offer a distinct, valuable service to the K–12 education community.

Tools for Surveying User Needs

Besides surveying the current collection of AskA services, it is important to gather information from or about the potential user community to make sure that there is a need for a particular type of service. Obviously user needs will be monitored on an ongoing basis once the service is implemented (see Module 2: Planning and Module 6: Evaluating), but it is important to establish an initial purpose for the service based on identified needs. For instance, an organization may discover through research on educational standards that national civics standards for high school students imply understanding the importance of participating in a democratic society, but there are few resources that help students apply democratic concepts to their personal lives. This is good ammunition for an organization that is interested in setting up a service to connect high school students with civic organizations.

Some methods for researching initial user needs regarding certain subject areas include the following:

- Monitor educational or other appropriate e-mail discussion groups (listservs).[11]
- Provide a questionnaire on an organization's Web site or location. (For instance, a library contemplating an electronic reference service can provide a questionnaire at the reference desk to solicit feedback on the idea.)
- Hold focus groups, interviews, or synchronous electronic discussion with potential users (e.g., teachers, students, parents, etc.).
- Research educational literature and other resources (Web, etc.) to establish educational trends in a particular subject area.
- Research national or regional standards for education.

Engaging in such activities and gathering user information allows organizations to be more prepared in the planning stages and assures that ideas for service are valid and useful.

---

[11] For a list of some educational listservs, see the AskERIC Education Listserv Archive *http://askeric.org/Virtual/Listserv_Archive/*

Work Sheet 1-1: Survey of AskA Environment

This page is available for you to record information as you research user needs and existing AskA service subject areas. The questions below are intended to facilitate your research and decision-making but do not account for all issues and questions that may arise during this process. Please feel free to record any additional ideas on a separate sheet of paper.

AskA Service Characteristics

1. Service type:

_____ K-12 curriculum area: _____

_____ Other topic area: _____

_____ General reference

2. Intended service users (check as many as apply):

_____ K-12 Students

_____ K-12 Educator/Administrator

_____ Parent of K-12 students

_____ General Public

_____ Other: _____

3. Stakeholders (individuals or organizations with an interest in service success):

_____ K-12 Students

_____ K-12 Educator

_____ Parent of K-12 students

_____ General Public

_____ Other: _____

User Needs Survey

1. Survey audience (stakeholders):

2. Primary survey questions:

3. Survey methods:

_____ Listservs, electronic discussion groups

_____ Survey (mail, phone, e-mail)

_____ Informal discussions with stakeholders

_____ Literature research

_____ Review of academic standards/curriculum areas

_____ Other: _____

4. Results

_____ There appears to be overall interest in proposed service.

_____ There appears to be some interest in proposed service.

_____ There does not appear to be any interest in proposed service.

5. Comments (including ideas for alternate direction of proposed service):

AskA Service Areas

1. Sources of existing AskA Services:

_____ AskA+ Locator *http://www.vrd.org/locator/subject.html*

_____ Web search (search by topic using Web search engines)

_____ People (K-12 community and others)

_____ Other sources:_____

2. Results

_____ There is a significant number of high quality AskA services in area of proposed service.

_____ There are some high quality AskA services in area of proposed service.

_____ There are no high quality AskA services in area of proposed service.

3. Comments (including ideas for alternate direction of proposed service):

Module 1 Summary

This section provided an introduction to the field of digital reference, including types of existing AskA services, general trends and issues, and tools for researching existing AskA services and potential user needs.

- Digital reference services (also referred to as AskA services) are Internet-based question-and-answer services that connect users with individuals who possess specialized subject or skill expertise. Many of these users are from the K–12 education community (e.g., students, educators, parents, etc.).

- Digital reference service affects different communities in different ways:

  1. Members of the library community have instituted digital reference as a means of providing additional and more convenient access to resources for library patrons within and beyond the local community. Digital reference represents a change in traditional reference service (librarians' roles, access to information, etc.).
  2. Members of the education community have benefited from subject and skill expertise provided by AskA services.
  3. Members of the business community use work-flow software such as help desks and call centers to provide person-to-person connections with clients and employees.

- Current quality AskA services focus heavily on the subjects of science and general reference but are lacking in areas such as art, history, literature, foreign language, and world geography.

- AskA services face several common issues including increasing question load, liability, confidentiality, software development, funding, publicity, staff recruitment and management, policy development, and resource development.

- K–12 digital reference services can consider 12 "Facets of Quality" in creating and maintaining service.

- Information about existing AskA services for K–12 education can be found by using the AskA+ Locator database of high-quality AskA services.

- Information on user needs can be gathered through a variety of methods, including electronic discussion groups, questionnaires, interviews, and literature research.

AskA Overviews

The following overviews offer surveys of the digital reference field in the subject areas of art and paleontology. They are provided as examples of research conducted to support the creation or ongoing work of AskA services in certain subject areas. These are models of good AskA research. See *www.vrd.org/AskA/digests.html* for these and other "AskA Digests," brief reports on current topics of interest to AskA services and users. (All URLs were current as of 1 November 98.)

Report of Art and Art Education AskA Services

Joann M. Wasik
Virtual Reference Desk
April 8, 1998

The State of Art-Related AskA Services

Despite the proliferation of AskA services, many subject areas remain inadequately represented with few or no services in effect. For example, while users seeking information from scientists or reference librarians have several services from which to choose, those seeking art and art education information find very few services available. The Virtual Reference Desk *(http://www.vrd.org)* has identified the following digital reference services that answer questions in different art-related areas; however, the scope and capabilities of these services differ widely.

Art and Art Education

National Museum of American Art Reference Desk
http://nmaa-ryder.si.edu/referencedesk/
This service both answers questions and provides information referral to its users within five business days. The scope is comprehensive and includes categories such as traditional fine arts, decorative arts and crafts, architecture and landscape design, photography, film and video, and commercial and graphic design. The service provides information on American art only.

Art Studio Chalkboard

http://www.saumag.edu/art/studio/chalkboard.html

This question-and-answer service functions primarily as a resource for artists and art students with questions regarding artistic technique (e.g., perspective, color, shading, etc.). Operated by a faculty member in Southern Arkansas University's art department, the service will occasionally answer art-related questions on other topics, but does not encourage out-of-scope questions. Question response time varies from several days to two months.

Metropolitan Museum of Art

http://wwar.com/cgi-bin/bbs/BBS/bbs_entrance.cgi

The Absolutely Arts Visual Arts Forum is an online bulletin board/discussion list where users post questions to be answered by other users. Since this service is not a true AskA service in that any user may respond to inquiries, differing opinions may prove to be confusing for some users seeking information, and some answers may be of questionable value.

Other Art-Related AskA Services

Photography

Wolf Camera & Video's Ask the Experts

http://wolfcamera.com/cgi-bin/wolf-conf/login

Formerly Online Photography Workshop's AskA Question Service, Wolf Camera and Video offers forums on several areas related to photography and video, including cameras, darkrooms, and other photographic equipment. The service is for questions relating to photographic equipment and techniques, and does not provide information on photographers or photographic works. Most forums are moderated, and many of the questions posted are answered by Wolf Camera staff. Note: Wolf Camera's service is just one example of AskA services that answer photographic and photographic equipment questions.

Architecture

There are several Ask an Architect sites on the Internet. Some are fee-based services, while others are clearly geared towards clients. Some free services are listed below.

Ask an Architect

http://www.askanarchitect.com/askme.html

This service is the volunteer effort of architect Parvin Gillim. Although the majority of his questions come from users involved in "do-it-yourself" projects, he does occasionally answer questions from K–12 classes. Most questions receive replies within a week, although the service has had few inquiries of late; a faulty Web form for question submission may have been a factor in the recent lack of questions.

Ask an Architect

http://infopoint.theriver.com/aiasac/ask_post.htm

Sponsored by the Southern Arizona Chapter American Institute of Architects, this online discussion forum appears to have been created as a resource for architects to share information with their colleagues. With eight messages posted since the forum's inception 13 months ago, the forum is little used, and does not appear to answer questions from the general public.

Conclusion

With the exception of the National Museum of American Art Reference Desk, and given the uncertain status of Ask A Question at the University of Auckland, there appear to be no other available resources for users with visual-arts-related questions at this time. There are no available services, for example, to answer questions regarding European or Asian art. While several art-related listservs and newsgroups are available to the general population over the Internet, any user may post replies to queries for information. As a result, any information obtained from these sources may be of questionable value.

Due to the lack of digital reference services in subject areas such as art, the information needs of many users may be left unmet. Moreover, a potential burden may be placed on the few services that do exist in underrepresented subject areas, as the question volume may prove to be overwhelming for too few services to effectively manage.

Report of Paleontology AskA Services

Joann M. Wasik
Virtual Reference Desk
June 28, 1998

Dinosaurs and Paleontology on the Internet

What is it about dinosaurs? The ancient reptiles flourished for 160 million years until their relatively sudden demise 65 million years ago. Yet the fascination with dinosaurs endures and continues to captivate the human imagination in children and adults alike.

There is a wealth of information about dinosaurs on the Internet, ranging from trivia about the Flintstones' pet Dino to the latest news on the links between dinosaurs and modern-day birds. Many of these sites receive thousands of hits per day, as the public interest in dinosaurs and their habitats persists. Despite the extensive number of dinosaur-related Web sites, however, there are relatively few sites that answer user questions about dinosaurs and other paleontology-related subjects.

The Virtual Reference Desk (*http://www.vrd.org*) has identified the following digital reference services that answer questions relating to dinosaurs; however, the scope and capabilities of these services differ widely. It should be noted that services focusing on other paleontological areas, such as paleobiology, botany, and fossils, are not included in the following resource list.

Dinosaur AskA Services

Ask-A-Geologist (USGS)
http://geology.usgs.gov/ask-a-geo.html

A service of the United States Geological Survey, this site answers questions on all aspects of geology, including paleontology. Since this service presently lacks the ability to keep subject-specific statistics, it is difficult to estimate how many dinosaur inquiries are received and answered.

Ask Mike!

http://www.gl.umbc.edu/~tkeese1/dinosaur/askmike.htm

Part of the Dinosaur Web pages, this question-and-answer service is hosted by a college student at the University of Maryland. The service currently receives between 3 and 10 questions a week, and users may have to wait up to six months to receive a reply.

Ask the Paleontologist

http://www.tyrrellmuseum.com/paleo.html

Slated to be unveiled in the summer of 1998, this new service is offered by the Royal Tyrrell Museum in Alberta, Canada. Questions will be answered by museum staff, and possibly international scientists as well.

The Dino Mall

http://www.trib.com/WYOMING/DINO/mall.html

Part of the Wyoming Dinosaur Center and Big Horn Basin Foundation, this service provides answers to questions by the Wyoming Dinosaur Center geologists. The service currently receives an average of 6–7 questions per week, and answers 100% in 1–2 days. All users receive personal replies from the service. Although currently static, the site is undergoing a total redesign to be completed in fall 1998. The service expects its question volume to increase significantly once the new, interactive site is launched.

Dino Russ's Lair

http://www.isgs.uiuc.edu/isgsroot/dinos/dinos_home.html

Dino Russ's Lair is a volunteer effort of Russell Jacobson at the Illinois State Geological Survey. The service receives approximately 30–40 questions per week. Attempts are made to answer all questions that require short, simple answers, and response time generally ranges from one week to one month, depending on Jacobson's availability.

Dinosaur Interplanetary Gazette: Dino Dish

http://www.InsideTheWeb.com/messageboard/mbs.cgi/mb29768

Hosted by an online magazine of dinosaur news and information, Dino Dish is an online message board where users post questions to be answered by other users. Since this service is not a true AskA service in that any user may respond to inquiries, differing opinions may prove to be confusing for some users seeking information, and some answers may be of questionable value. Dinosaur Interplanetary Gazette also sponsors a special monthly Ask a Paleontologist message board service with notable guest paleontologists such as Jack Horner.

E-mail the Curator (The Worldwide Museum of Natural History)
http://www.wmnh.com/wmvd0000.htm

E-mail the Curator is a commercial site, which receives hundreds of questions about dinosaurs from users each week. Only a few questions are responded to due to large question volume.

The MAD Scientist Network
http://madsci.wustl.edu/

MAD Scientist answers questions in many areas of science, including earth science. The service does not receive many inquiries for dinosaur information, and estimates that perhaps less than 1% of all questions received are dinosaur-related.

Paleo Forum
http://www.pitt.edu/~mattf/PaleoForumInfo.html

This service is a message board for discussions on paleontology, paleoanthropology, prehistoric archeology, evolutionary biology, and the evolution of behavior. Many of the topics on the discussion board tend to be rather technical in nature, and may not be suitable for many K–12 students or laypeople. As with all message board-style forums, differing opinions may prove to be confusing for some users seeking information, and some answers may be of questionable value.

ScienceNet
http://www.sciencenet.org.uk/first.html

ScienceNet is a service that answers questions relating to science, technology, engineering, and medicine. At this writing, there are approximately 60 archived answers to questions relating to dinosaurs. The service does not receive dinosaur questions on a consistent basis, but rather in "fits and starts," particularly after the release of dinosaur-related film productions such as *Jurassic Park*.

Scientific American: Ask the Experts
http://www.sciam.com/askexpert/index.html

An online companion to the popular print journal, Scientific American offers a question-and-answer service in several different areas of science, including geology. There are very few archived question-and-answer sets regarding paleontology, and it appears that the service does not receive many inquiries for dinosaur information. Inquiries as to the volume and scope of dinosaur questions received by the service have remained unanswered to date.

There are also dinosaur-related newsgroups and listservs such as the Dinosaur mailing list (*dinosaur@usc.edu*) at the University of Southern California, which works in conjunction with the Cleveland Museum of Natural History. Although paleontologists do respond to user questions via the listserv, public forums such as mailing lists cannot necessarily guarantee subscribers authoritative or timely replies to their queries. Other sites run special, time-limited services that are tied to specific events. To coincide with an expedition in the Gobi desert in 1997, the Discovery Channel Online hosted a "Dinosaur in the Dunes" question-and-answer service where users could e-mail questions to the expedition team. Question-and-answer sets from the expedition are available at *http://www.discovery.com/area/specials/gobi/e-mailreply.html*, although the service ceased operation when the expedition ended in August 1997, and no longer accepts questions.

As illustrated in the above resource list, some AskA services are overrun with requests for paleontology information while others receive relatively few questions. It is possible that users are unaware of the paleontology and dinosaur resources at some services; this seems particularly apparent in the case of services that answer questions in multiple areas of science, such as the MAD Scientist Network. Instead, users seem to rely primarily on sites that are explicit in their dinosaur focus, such as Dino Russ's Lair and the E-mail the Curator service at the Worldwide Museum of Natural History. As a result, these latter services receive a high volume of questions and can answer only a fraction of the questions received.

The demand for dinosaur information continues to grow unabated, and some AskA services have been forced to cease operations due to unmanageable question loads. The University of California (Berkeley) Museum of Paleontology discontinued their popular PaleoPals message board service in early June 1998 due to question overload and the lack of qualified staff to answer questions. As many inquiries required additional research by the paleontologists, and few questions lent themselves to becoming part of a Frequently Asked Questions (FAQ) document, the service was unable to keep up with user demand.

Digital reference and AskA services are valuable resources that support the teaching and learning efforts of the K–12 community and beyond. As more services exceed their capacity to effectively and efficiently answer all questions received, many users' information needs are left unmet. The creation of new AskA services, along with increased communication among existing services, may serve to promote shared resources and information. Such a cooperative effort may result in distributed question loads and increased rates of response to users, and thus provide more effective and timely information delivery.

Module 2

Informing
Planning
Training
Prototyping
Contributing
Evaluating

Planning

Creating a Plan for Building and Maintaining an AskA Service

Module Profile

This module is designed to help organizations design a plan for building and delivering an AskA service that best represents organization goals. This module discusses issues in planning, including the general structure of AskA services, and illustrates through case studies the experiences of exemplary services. An AskA Plan work sheet is included to help new AskA services organize necessary service components. At the conclusion of this module, you will be able to achieve the following goal:

Goal   Determine the best way to build and maintain a digital reference service within a given organization.

Prerequisites   Before developing and implementing an AskA plan, you should be able to collect information on the general digital reference field and existing AskA services (see Module 1: Informing).

Objectives   At the completion of this module, you will be able to achieve the following objectives:
1. Identify service goals that are consistent with those of supporting organization(s).
2. State components of general structure of AskA services.
3. Create and implement an "AskA plan" for new service.
4. Apply general structure to individual service.
5. Review plans of exemplary AskA services to identify important service components.

41

2.1 Creating and Implementing the AskA Plan

The AskA plan is a document that outlines the potential components of a particular AskA service. The plan is based on a generalized structure of AskA services and reflects the overall goals of the service and its supporting organization(s). This section discusses issues in developing service goals, understanding the general AskA service structure, and implementing an AskA plan.

Service Goals

In order to create an initial plan for the development and implementation of a new AskA service, it is necessary to establish service goals that are consistent with goals of the supporting organization(s) (e.g., library, academic institution, professional association, government agency, etc.). It is important to recognize that an AskA service can provide many benefits to its supporting organization(s). By promoting consistent goals, AskA services can serve as another vehicle to reach those goals.

Digital Reference Service as Part of Larger Organization

Most digital reference services do not exist independently. They are an integral part of a larger system: university program, professional association, government agency, etc. The digital reference component of an organization frequently operates under the organization's mission, goals, and objectives.

The organization and its digital reference service can share a symbiotic relationship. The digital reference service may receive financial or operational support from an organization, although it is common for a service to seek outside funding and support as well. The organization benefits from the relationship in important ways including the following:

- **Feedback to improve organization.** By offering direct human interaction, a digital reference service can help the organization monitor user and stakeholder needs. Information from digital reference transactions can help the organization develop and improve resources and services (Lankes, 1995).

- **Promotion of national initiatives.** Participation in digital reference service allows organizations and individuals to serve as volunteers through mentoring in response to President Clinton's call for increased volunteerism (White House, 1997) and to carry out Vice President Gore's online tutoring initiative to connect students to "a national network of top experts" (White House, 1998, Online).

- **Impact on education.** Digital reference service offers the opportunity to become directly involved in K–12 education by serving as an important component in student learning and professional development of educators.

Writing Service Goals

When writing service goals, the following questions should be considered:

- Who are the audiences of the service (both immediate and peripheral)?
- What will members of the audience gain from using the service?
- What will the greater organization and stakeholders gain from offering the service?
- What will staff gain from participating in the service?

One area that some services for K–12 students may want to explore is national or regional educational standards and benchmarks in order to target specific known areas of the curriculum[12].

Examples of Service Goals

Below are examples of service goals as they may be stated for two different types of services.

Goals of general subject AskA service for K–12 students, where teachers serve as experts:

1. Motivate students to learn.
2. Guide students in conducting research effectively.
3. Help students improve written communications skills.
4. Help teachers become proficient Internet users.

Goals of electronic library reference service for K–12 students and adults, where professional librarians respond to user questions.[13]

1. Provide quality information service and resources to the public.
2. Create quality information resources on the Internet.
3. Promote the roles of librarians in the information age.

---

[12] For information on educational standards, see "Content Knowledge" from Mid-continent Regional Educational Laboratory (McREL) *http://www.mcrel.org/standards-benchmarks/* and "Developing Educational Standards" from Putnam Valley Central Schools *http://www.putwest.boces.org/Standards.html.*

[13] Also see The Internet Public Library Mission Statement *http://www.ipl.org/about/newmission.html*

These types of goals can help guide the digital reference service in decision making and development of the service. However, a list of goals is only one of many components in the AskA plan. The following section discusses a general structure of AskA services that can be used to guide new services in establishing components within a plan.

AskA Anatomy

After the main goals are identified to help guide the creation and management of the service, decisions should be made regarding plans to reach the goals using the suggested AskA framework as discussed below. The AskA Plan should outline the planned resources, activities, and products of the service based on this general structure of AskA services.

General Components: The AskA Anatomy

All AskA services can be described in terms of a conceptual framework with three main components: detectors, rules, and effectors. Each of the three components represents the many roles, relationships, activities, resources, products, etc. involved in building and maintaining an AskA service. The components are described and outlined below.

This structure is based on research of six exemplary digital reference services.[14] See Table 2-2 for a more detailed breakdown of components.

Detectors. Detectors are the organization's mechanisms for acquiring information on the environment. The knowledge gained through detector activities can help ensure that the service meets user and stakeholder needs and uses the most efficient processes and tools. Detectors can gain information about the following:

- Users—general public, specifically members of K–12 community (students, parents, educators)
- Other Internet information services—existing AskA services, general Internet information services, etc.
- Application builders—developers of software programs that run on the Internet (user interfaces, etc.): Web browsers, servers, other software (e.g., animation, real-time audio, etc.)
- Infrastructure providers—technology used to make network connections (leased lines, bridges, routers, modems, etc.), standards regarding technology, etc.
- Internal sources—service staff, participants (e.g., information specialists/experts, etc.)
- External sources—funders, overseeing organizations/institutions, etc.

---

[14] For more complete discussion of AskA service structure and related research, see Lankes (1998). The terms **detectors**, **rules**, and **effectors** used by Lankes (1998) were developed by John Holland of the University of Michigan.

Information from these sources helps form the AskA's "view of the world" and forms the foundation for all decisions about how the service is built and maintained.

Rules. Rules represent the actions of an AskA service based on the information from detectors. Types of rules include question-answering, routing, archiving, resource-building, etc. Since rules are abstract with no physical structure, resources must be used to actually carry out the actions. Resources—people, software, hardware, etc.—are the means of implementing rules.

Human Resources. While the number of staff or volunteers in a service can vary (as do specific job titles and number of people performing each task), there are several job roles or tasks that are common to many AskA services. It also varies as to which roles (if any) are paid positions as opposed to volunteer efforts. Below are some common roles or tasks and some titles associated with them:

- Manage the daily operations of service (e.g., administrator, coordinator, technical staff, programmers)
- Institute policy and research areas for further development (e.g. director, administrator, coordinator)
- Respond to user queries (e.g., information specialists, experts, volunteers)
- Oversee performance of those who respond to queries (if different from titles mentioned in 1 and 2, can be mentors, trainers, team leaders).

Technical Resources. These types of resources include Web servers and electronic mail for carrying out question-answering, archiving, and other processes. Table 2-1 shows examples of technical resources as they correspond with service rules.

Table 2-1 Service Rules and Technical Resources

Rules	Technical Resources
Establish Web presence	server space, connection, etc.
Receive incoming questions and feedback from users	e-mail, Web form
Respond to users	can be individual e-mail account or Web page
Route questions to potential respondents	database, e-mail account
Archive previously asked questions	database, search engine, etc.
Make available supporting information resources	Web page (can include search engines, graphics, etc.)

Effectors. Effectors are sets of services offered to users or others on the Internet in order to meet reference needs. This can include the ultimate question-answer service, supporting information in the form of a Web site (archives, frequently asked questions

[FAQs], references to other resources), phone service, special events, etc. Effectors are the output of an AskA service. These mechanisms are an organization's means of changing the world around it—or at least its own place in it.

Table 2-2 outlines the three components—detectors, rules, effectors—in terms of their subcomponents (detectors are broken down by agents of information) and provides examples based on practices of existing services. The examples do not represent a complete sample of AskA components, but provide some ideas for organizations getting started.

Table 2-2 AskA Service Structure and Common Components

Component	Agent/Subcomponent	Examples
Detector	Users	• User surveys/feedback forms • Archive of e-mail interactions • Web server logs • Focus groups
	Internet Information Services	• Web browsing for other Internet information services • Formal review, collection, and analysis of data
	Internet Application Builders	• Trade journals • Web sites with software reviews, information
	Internet Infrastructure Providers	Information and experience with • Bandwidth • Routing/switching • TCP/IP
	Internal Influences	• Employee ideas
	External Influences	• Funders • Marketing concerns • Needs of larger organization
Rules	Detector Information Process	• Prioritize incoming information • Translate information into process (via meetings)
	Process	• Question answering • Triage of questions • Archiving questions and responses • Modification/development
	Resource Types	• Hardware/software tools • People • Policies • Information resources (used in question answering)
	Resource Types (people)	• Roles (administrative/question-routing, question answering, technical, research, etc.) • Skills
	Effector Tie-Ins	• Policies for modifying existing services/creating new services
Effectors	Technical	• Web site—question form, archive, FAQ • Gopher site • FTP site • E-mail service
	Other	• Toll-free telephone number • Multiple Web sites • Workshops/conferences

Meta-Description

From looking at exemplary digital reference services,[15] the basic structure of AskA
services can be described in a single abstract meta-description as seen in Figure 2-1. This
figure follows a blueprint format and may be read left to right. The leftmost column
represents detectors (Question Acquisition, Web Surfing, Publications, Parent
Organization). These are mechanisms universally used by exemplary services to gather
information for an AskA service. A single question-answer process is used to process
incoming questions and is outlined below. The single effector listed in this abstract meta-
description, "Answer Sent to User via E-Mail," is inverted. (See Appendix A for sample
blueprints of exemplary AskA services.)

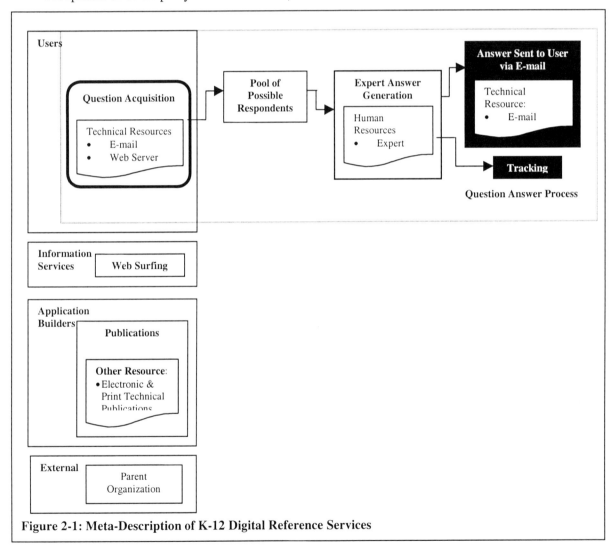

Figure 2-1: Meta-Description of K-12 Digital Reference Services

---

[15] See companion research report "Building and Maintaining Internet Information Services: K–12 Digital
Reference Services" available from ERIC Clearinghouse on Information and Technology (Lankes, 1998).

This simple process covers the range of possible activities related to question-answering processes; this does not represent Web development activities, as they are common across the exemplary services researched in the companion research study. It also incorporates common resources and detectors from the exemplary services. Table 2-3 defines the steps in the "Question-Answer Process" of the meta-description.

Table 2-3: Components of the Meta-Description Question-Answer Process

Step	Description
Question Acquisition	An e-mail address or Web form is used to allow a user to enter a question. This may require the user to determine a topic for the question. Some automated preprocessing may occur to put the question in HTML or assign some sort of tracking identification.
Pool of Possible Respondents	A message is queued and prepared for expert response. In services with multiple experts available, some triage process occurs (for example, in Ask A Volcanologist a PERL script simply sends questions to experts based on the days of the week, while MAD Scientist Network uses moderators to select experts). In single-person operations, messages are simply queued for the single expert.
Expert Answer Is Generated	An expert generates an answer. In some services this is done in accordance with a policy document. In some services these answers come from Internet resources, and in all cases the expert has personal knowledge of the topic.
Answer Sent to User via E-Mail	Once an answer is generated, it is sent to the user via e-mail (if possible).
Tracking	Trends and subjects from questions are tracked and used. In some cases the trends are used in Web development. Tracking can consist of Web-based archive, private archive, or simply informal information.

Simply put, a question is received through the Web or e-mail. A process determines the best expert to answer the question. Once an appropriate expert has been identified, that expert formulates an answer. The answer is sent to the user via e-mail. After an answer has been created a tracking process occurs. In some cases this involves the creation of a public Web-searchable archive. Other services use a private archive. Still others use a more informal tracking process to inform the creation of Web resources.

Implementing the AskA Plan

Once the components are outlined and a general plan is formed, the service can start implementing the plan: establishing processes, hiring staff, acquiring resources, etc. It should be noted that many existing services have entered into operations (rules) and service provision (effectors) without mapping out an original detailed plan. While this approach can result in quality service, a new service can save time and make more consistent decisions when guided by a general structure as outlined in this module.

2.2 Creating Your Own AskA Plan

This section offers a work sheet with a list of questions to guide new services in creating an AskA plan. Using the questions from the work sheet, the meta-description can be tuned and expanded to meet the needs of your organization.

Work Sheet 2-1: Questions to Guide the AskA Plan

Conceptual Framework Section	Sub Section	Questions	Considerations/ Suggestions	Answers/Comments
Detector	Internet Agent Type (Users)	• How will you keep track of your users? • What type of information will you attempt to gather about users of your services? • What specific mechanisms will you put in place to gather this information?	• Determine number of users. • Determine demographics of users. • Use logs (such as logs from a World Wide Web server). • Keep archives of e-mail interactions. • Provide online feedback forms. • Conduct focus groups.	
Detector	Internet Agent Type (Information Services)	• What will you keep track of regarding other K–12 digital reference services? • What will you keep track of with other Internet information services in general? • How will you gather ideas from other Internet sites and incorporate them into your own services? • What specific mechanisms will you put in place to gather this information?	• Surf the Web. • Decide whether or not to assign specific responsibilities to yourself or staff regarding reviewing other sites, doing digital reference, or building Internet sites. • Allot time to review other sites on the Internet.	
Detector	Internet Agent Type (Application Builders)	• How will you keep current on software available on the Internet (e.g., Web browsers)? • How will you determine new trends in software (e.g., real-time media like RealAudio)? • How will you determine what software to acquire for your K–12 digital reference service? • What specific mechanisms will you put in place to gather this information?	• Use logs to determine the type of software being used to access your site. • Query users about their technical setup. • Check certain Web sites for software- specific updates. • Develop relations with vendors specifically to "keep ahead" of the changing Internet software. • Read trade journals for current trends and software news.	

Conceptual Framework Section	Sub Section	Questions	Considerations/Suggestions	Answers/Comments
Detectors	Internet Agent Type (Infrastructure Providers)	• How will your service connect to the Internet? • Who will be primarily in charge of this relationship? • How will you monitor changes in your connection? • How will you stay aware of standards-setting processes such as the Internet Engineering Task Force? • What specific mechanisms will you put in place to gather this information?	• Determine type of bandwidth that will be available to your service. • Consider technologies such as routing and switching in decisions regarding how you build and maintain your services. • Consider TCP/IP issues.	
Detectors	Internal Influences	• How will you capture ideas generated from those working on your service? • Will you consider employee ideas in determining how the service is run? • What specific mechanisms will you put in place to gather this information?	• Identify staff members to act as innovators. • Identify individual(s) to set the vision for the organization.	

Detectors	External Influences	• How will forces outside of the Internet affect your service?
		• What non-Internet sources of information will inform how to build and maintain your service?
		• What specific mechanisms will you put in place to gather this information?
			• Consider:
			  • Funder influence on day-to-day service agenda.
			  • Influence of larger marketing or systems concerns.
			• Determine the needs of the larger organization in terms of your service.	

Rules	Detector Information Processing	• How will you prioritize the information acquired from the Internet, internal sources, and external sources? • How will this information link into your daily procedures?	• Consider priority by *type* of information (such as users)? • Hold daily or weekly meetings to discuss what's happening outside of the organization.	

Conceptual Framework Section	Sub Section	Questions	Considerations/ Suggestions	Answers/Comments
Rules	Process	• How will you answer the questions of the K–12 community? • How will you gather and distribute questions and then ensure users get answers?	• Use volunteers to answer questions. • Determine method for archiving questions. • Determine methods for modifying existing service or creating new services.	
Rules	Resource Types	• What hardware and software tools will you use to build and maintain your service? • How many people will be involved within the organization in the digital reference service? • What policies will you put in place to guide the operation of this service?	• Use the Web to answer the K–12 education community's questions (or e-mail or other Internet tools). • Consider hardware requirements involved in conducting this service.	
Rules	Resource Types (People)	• What skills are required of the people who build and maintain this service? • Will the people processing the questions have high technical skills? • Will they have library backgrounds?	• Identify roles in service processes. • Identify roles of different people. • Determine whether or not there is a need to distinguish between those who process the questions (intermediaries) and those who answer the questions (the collection).	
Rules	Effector Tie-Ins	• What policies or decision-making structures will you put in place for modifying your existing services or creating new services?	• Consider stakeholders' expectations (such as users or funders).	
Effectors	Technical	• What types of Internet tools will be used to deliver information to the K–12 community?	Provide: • Web site • Gopher site • FTP site	
Effectors	Other	• What other types of services will you offer to the K–12 community?	Provide: • Toll-free telephone number • Multiple Web sites • Workshops or conferences	

2.3 Examples and Experiences in Planning AskA Services

This section offers case studies of three exemplary K–12 digital reference services (Ask Dr. Math, MAD Scientist Network, and National Museum of American Art Reference Desk) in order to provide ideas and help organizations get started on their AskA Plans. Appendix A includes "blueprints" of each service's framework in terms of its detectors, rules, and effectors. The case studies and blueprints highlight K–12 AskA services that are considered top quality according to criteria established by the Virtual Reference Desk (see "Facets of Quality" in Module 1).

Planning AskA Services: In Their Own Words

The following case studies describe experiences of three exemplary digital reference services. An administrator from each AskA service, offers information and advice regarding issues in the initial planning process as well as ongoing service development. Blueprints for each service (as described above) are included in Appendix A. The case studies include the following:

- "The Evolution of Ask Dr. Math" by Ken Williams and Steve Weimar describes three phases of growth over the more than three years of math reference service.

- "Getting Underway: The Virtual Reference Desk at the National Museum of American Art" by Joan Stahl discusses the history, mission, and usage trends of this art information service along with lessons learned after five years of service.

- "Planning an Ask-A-Scientist Service" by Lynn Bry shares questions faced during the development of this science question-answer service for K–12 students.

Case Study

The Evolution of "Ask Dr. Math"

by Ken Williams and Stephen Weimar

The Math Forum's question-and-answer service, "Ask Dr. Math," has undergone a great evolution since it began in 1994. From its inception through April 1998, Ask Dr. Math has taken on over 225 volunteer "doctors" from all corners of the globe. The service continues to grow in popularity and has received a number of Internet awards. Our "About Ask Dr. Math" page provides more information:

http://forum.swarthmore.edu/dr.math/abt.drmath.html

Our specific evolutionary process may be of interest to people who wish to start their own question-and-answer services. In general, our growth can be divided into three main phases of development. These phases reflect periods of self-definition, expansion, and enhancement.

Phase 1: Launching the service, evolving standards for quality
(November 1994–December 1995)

When we launched our service in November 1994, a small group of Swarthmore College students volunteered their time to answer math questions received from K–12 students around the world. We didn't advertise our services very widely, since our staff was small and had limited time. Initially we simply posted the following announcement to several math-oriented discussion groups on the Internet, including "geometry-pre-college" and "sci.math":

```
┌─────────────────────────────────────────────────┐
│                   Ask Dr. Math                    │
│                                                   │
│              Have a math question?                │
│     No problem you're working on is to big or     │
│                    too small.                     │
│    Want to talk to someone who loves math?        │
│         Let's do some math together!              │
│                  Write to:                        │
│            Dr.math@forum.swarthmore.edu           │
└─────────────────────────────────────────────────┘
```

```
If you are a student in elementary, middle,
or high school, write to us!  We can't wait
to help you with those really tough or
interesting problems.  All of the Ask Dr.
Math letters are answered by members of "The
Swat Team," math students and professors here
at Swarthmore College (and some famous
"ringers" from elsewhere in the math world,
including John Conway at Princeton).  Ask Dr.
Math is a project of the GEOMETRY FORUM, an
NSF-funded program housed at Swarthmore
College in Swarthmore, Pennsylvania, USA.

Dr. Math is not a mailing-list, it's an e-
mail address that you can write to with math
questions, and we'll write you back.  If you
write to us, please include a subject in your
message that says something about your
question.
```

At this stage, Dr. Math was just an e-mail alias; any mail sent to *dr.math@forum.swarthmore.edu* was forwarded to the entire list of volunteers. When we answered questions, we copied our responses to the list.

During this phase, we kept certain key questions in mind about how we wanted the service to grow and develop. Some of the more important concerns were the following:

1. What kind of service do we want to be? A homework help service? A reference service? An interactive tutoring service?
2. What distinguishes a helpful answer from an unhelpful one?
3. Will we try to answer all the questions we get? If not, which ones will we choose?

It has been quite useful to keep these questions in mind throughout the evolution of our service. The answers to these questions could determine very different paths for a question-and-answer service. For instance, if a project chooses to be a homework help service (which is NOT what we chose as our primary mission), the project's highest priorities should probably include immediate answering and coordination with teachers.

Phase 1 Questions and Answers

You may want to look at some interactions from the first phase of Dr. Math:

http://forum.swarthmore.edu/dr.math/problems/1_0_not_prime.html
http://forum.swarthmore.edu/dr.math/problems/pi_irrational_numbers.html
http://forum.swarthmore.edu/dr.math/problems/purpose_zero.html
http://forum.swarthmore.edu/dr.math/problems/addition.html
http://forum.swarthmore.edu/dr.math/problems/adding_pets.html
http://forum.swarthmore.edu/dr.math/problems/solving_hard_way.html
http://forum.swarthmore.edu/dr.math/problems/circle_chords.html
http://forum.swarthmore.edu/dr.math/problems/collinear.html

Phase 2: Building an archive, incorporating outside volunteers, implementing standards
(January 1996 – March 1997)

It didn't take long for us to realize that a great many people had math questions. We needed to find a way to expand the scope of our service. To do this, we asked ourselves other questions:

1. What do we like most about our service?
2. What technical aspects of our answering process need to improve?

We also began to develop answers to some of the Phase 1 questions concerning the service's character and issues of quality as we gained experience with our service and learned more about the needs of the community we served. These answers helped us choose directions in which to expand.

Question-Answer Management

First, we needed to improve coordination among the volunteers and to save their personal e-mail accounts from the deluge of Dr. Math–related messages. To accomplish these goals, we wrote a software package called The *Doctor's Office* in the summer of 1995 to manage the flow of questions and answers. This Web-based package included a "Triage" area where our volunteers could choose a question to answer, a "Post-Op" area where volunteers could review each other's work, and environments to view and answer questions. The software sent answers to users via e-mail.

Incorporating Outside Volunteers

Second, we decided that in order to answer more questions and broaden our range of expertise, we needed to enlist the help of volunteers from outside the Swarthmore College community. To do this, we had to develop a training and review process for our new volunteers. We based this process in a new area in the *Doctor's Office* called the "Holding Tank," where answers from our volunteers-in-training could be reviewed by more experienced volunteers before being sent to the questioner.

Defining the Service

We decided that we would not be a homework help service, because homework problems typically need to be answered within a matter of hours. Our project relied on volunteers to answer questions, and we didn't want to ask them to be "on call" to answer questions immediately. We also decided that our primary role was not that of a reference service, since several good mathematics reference services already existed on the Internet. Also, our volunteers seemed more interested in actually doing math problems and helping students with math concepts than in referring them to other sources of help.

Building the Archive

We realized that simply increasing the number of volunteers wouldn't be enough to combat the growing number of questions. Furthermore, our project was administered primarily by volunteer Swarthmore students who would not have time to train all the new volunteers needed. We also realized that we were beginning to build up an archive of mathematics information that had value in its own right and that we could take advantage of this resource in answering questions as well. Thus we decided to shift our focus to building our archive of previously answered questions.

Once we made this shift, we realized that it made sense for many reasons. First, many people asked questions that had already been answered well and were in the archive. If they could find and understand an appropriate answer in the archive, they might not need to ask the question at all; in fact their needs would be filled more quickly by looking in the archive than if they had to wait for a reply.

Second, many people benefit from seeing several different approaches to a problem. A typical response from a volunteer explains one way of doing a problem or may give just one example, whereas the archive can present many different views of similar questions. Exposure to a variety of approaches leads to a greater understanding of the mathematics and often to a realization that mathematics is not primarily a matter of finding the right recipe of calculations to perform. Indeed, we feel that one of the most valuable aspects of our service is that we can provide a very different way of looking at a problem than a student's teacher might.

Third, the archive allows us to focus more of our energy on questions we think are interesting, rather than answering the same kind of question many times. This helps our volunteers remain enthusiastic about participating in our project, and as a result they stay aboard longer and write more interesting answers.

During this emphasis on the archive, we were presented with some technical challenges. We needed a smooth process for generating and editing an archive and an intuitive means of accessing it for both the volunteer doctors and the public. Conceptually we had to design a structure for the archive that would meet the needs of a wide range of users. We chose to organize resources by grade level, and then within those levels by math topic, thinking that this structure would be most familiar to our young users.

Implementing Standards and Training Resources

When we had arrived at a more precise definition of our service, we were able to create a guide for our volunteers that helped them write responses. The guide contains technical information about making everything work properly as well as guidelines for writing clear, helpful responses. This has been a wonderful resource for our volunteers.

Phase 2 Questions and Answers

Here are some interactions from our second phase:

http://forum.swarthmore.edu/dr.math/problems/humphreys6.22.96.html
http://forum.swarthmore.edu/dr.math/problems/tao10.26.96.html
http://forum.swarthmore.edu/dr.math/problems/devo5.15.96.html
http://forum.swarthmore.edu/dr.math/problems/unknown4.17.96.html
http://forum.swarthmore.edu/dr.math/problems/georgia4.19.96.html
http://forum.swarthmore.edu/dr.math/problems/milburn5.29.96.html

You may wish to compare these with the interactions from the first phase. In general, you may find these more comprehensive and representative of more points of view. The tone of these responses may not be as enthusiastic as those of our eager college students who had the sense that they were helping *create* a new service rather than helping *sustain* a service.

Phase 3: Adding value to the archive and planning for the future
(April 1997–present)

From the first two phases, we have identified issues that guide our work and help us choose our priorities for future development. These priorities include the following:

- Facilitating mathematical satisfaction
- Managing increasing numbers of questions
- Maintaining a consistently high quality of interaction
- Leveraging the interactions so that many people may benefit from them
- Improving the question-submission process
- Maximizing the quality and use of our archive

During Phase 3, we are currently concentrating on adding value to our archive, educating users on how to effectively use the service, and creating new resources and processes for the future.

Adding Value to the Archive

To add value to our archive, we have assembled several Frequently Asked Question files that provide an overview of various topics (e.g., Pascal's Triangle, Pi) and provide links to good responses on these topics. Unlike our archive, these FAQ files are not organized around specific math problems; rather, they give richer, more comprehensive treatments of broad topics. FAQ files are created by collecting and organizing a number of different questions and answers as well as other related Internet resources. Our FAQ is located at *http://forum.swarthmore.edu/dr.math/faq/*

User Education (Communicating Effective Use of Service)

In managing the volume of questions we realized that we needed to improve the entry process, focusing on answering questions that are genuine, well-formed, and not readily answered elsewhere. To this end we now provide recommendations for teachers who want to use our service in a classroom situation and tell them what kinds of things are not considered effective use. Since we began providing these recommendations, inappropriate use of Dr. Math by teachers has decreased. Our recommendations are at *http://forum.swarthmore.edu/dr.math/approp.use.html.*

Planning for the Future

To further expand the capacity of our service, we have experimented with ways of setting up mentorships between new volunteers and more experienced "Math Doctors." Until now, most of our training has been done in a centralized manner with our administrators mentoring our new volunteers. The time required to interact with trainees has been our biggest bottleneck in terms of involving new volunteers in our project, and we would like to find effective alternatives without compromising the quality of our service.

We are also considering possibilities for "franchising," allowing others to set up local versions of Ask Dr. Math that have access to our experience, software, and central database. For example, a school district may want to set up a question-and-answer service in which students in the high schools answer questions from students in elementary schools.

As we continue to focus on supporting individual students interested in exploring and learning mathematics, we realize that the short, discrete questions and answers in the archive do not lend themselves to more extended investigations of topics. It is important that services such as ours be able to present their archive not as collections of discrete questions and answers but rather as more structured resources that present the inherent linkages and structure within their subject areas. Our FAQs help somewhat in this area, but we still feel that more support is needed.

Towards this end, one of our most talented volunteers is working with our support to develop a more coherent and multidimensional environment in which to explore math topics within the K–12 curriculum. This environment would allow a user to view several different perspectives on a given section of the Ask Dr. Math Web site (e.g., fractions); different math concepts will be explained through voices of teachers, peers, mathematicians, etc. This new resource will become an integral part of the Ask Dr. Math environment so that volunteers and questioners can use it as a source of information, and anyone using it can be connected to the question-submission form. The question-submission process will capture information regarding the specific resources (i.e., Web page) used by the questioner when submitting the question. This contextual information will enhance the processes of answering questions and managing the incoming queue.

Finally, we would like to create a question-asking environment in which people's questions are correlated programmatically with our archive, and submitters are directed to appropriate archive entries. There are many different ways we could implement this, and our challenge will be to find out which ways are effective. For instance, submitters could type in brief summaries of their questions, indicate which of our categories they might fall into, and press *submit*. The next page will include several items from our archive that match submitters' questions most closely. If they still want to ask their question, we will provide a form in which they could record the complete question.

Phase 3 Questions and Answers

Here are some examples of entries in our FAQ, including links to questions and answers from our most recent period of activity:

http://forum.swarthmore.edu/dr.math/faq/faq.order.operations.html
http://forum.swarthmore.edu/dr.math/faq/faq.negxneg.html
http://forum.swarthmore.edu/dr.math/faq/faq.sqrt.by.hand.html
http://forum.swarthmore.edu/dr.math/faq/faq.comb.perm.html
http://forum.swarthmore.edu/dr.math/faq/faq.doubling.pennies.html

Conclusion

As we look toward the future, we look to create new ways for users to interact with the Ask Dr. Math resources and experts in order to motivate learning and support basic goals of K–12 math curricula. With our rich set of resources and over three years' experience in answering student questions, we are confident that Ask Dr. Math will continue to support math education and pave new roads for digital reference.

Ken Williams, *ken@forum.swarthmore.edu,* is programmer and administrator for The Math Forum, and Stephen Weimar, *steve@forum.swarthmore.edu,* is the co-principal investigator of The Math Forum.

Planning an Ask-A-Scientist Service

by Lynn Bry

Introduction

The MAD Scientist Network (MadSci) *http://www.madsci.org* is a Web-based "Ask-A-Scientist Service" started in 1995 by Lynn Bry and Joe Simpson, both M.D./Ph.D. students at Washington University Medical School in St. Louis. The site began as a branch of the "Young Scientist Program" (YSP) (*medicine.wustl.edu/~ysp/*), a student-run program at the medical school that aims to increase the science literacy of local K–12 students through hands-on learning. We created the site to provide a means by which students at the local public schools could ask questions of the faculty, staff, and students at Washington University. Though our intentions were local, we were well aware that the nature of the Web provided worldwide exposure. However, we felt it best to initially target our efforts to a specific audience. More than two months of planning went into devising and creating the infrastructure for the site before it officially appeared on the Web. During this period the following questions were considered and addressed:

What technical resources would be needed?

Given that the service would exist on the Web, Web space was the primary requirement. The medical school provided Web space free of charge, including the ability to run CGI scripts and search engines specifically for the site.

Secondarily, personnel would be needed to create Web documents and CGI interfaces and to oversee the distribution of questions among experts. HTML and CGI scripting was undertaken by Lynn Bry, while Joe Simpson oversaw the basic administration of the site. We felt that CGI scripts would greatly facilitate the utility of the service by making information searchable, assisting the selection of scientists to answer questions, and assuming many of the time-consuming, mundane tasks such as formatting information with hypertext and generating listings of questions and answers.

Who would answer questions?

Forty scientists at the medical school volunteered to answer questions in response to fliers posted on campus. Their level of education ranged from full professors to graduate and medical students. An online form at the preliminary Web site allowed people to sign up. The form asked for basic information as well as the areas in which people wished to answer questions.

What areas of science would be targeted?

We based the areas on the primary areas of expertise at the medical school—the biological sciences and chemistry. The areas were divided into 20 "categories" (e.g., anatomy, biochemistry, chemistry, genetics, medicine, zoology, etc.).

How would questions and answers be received?

During 1995 many of the St. Louis schools had or were expected to have Internet access. Receipt of information through Web forms seemed the easiest and least labor-intensive method of receiving questions and answers. Information from Web forms could be easily processed by Perl CGI scripts to create HTML files. In this manner both questions and answers could be easily presented on the Web, providing an easy means to archive information. The use of the Web also fit nicely with other activities run by the YSP including a "Computer Literacy Team" that traveled to schools to teach teachers and students about using the Web in the classroom.

How would information be organized?

A series of "area codes" were created to specify the individual areas of science (anatomy = An; zoology = Zo). These codes corresponded with areas in which scientists could answer questions, thus providing a simple means of generating a pool of scientists to answer a given question. The codes are also used by CGI scripts to present listings of specific categories or to limit a keyword search to one or more areas.

Given that two individuals oversaw the workings of the site, we decided to do as much as we could using the Web; this included reviewing questions, sending material to scientists, and checking information in answers. A series of Web-form CGI scripts were written in Perl to carry out functions such as processing incoming questions and answers, generating listings of files on the fly, and providing a simple interface in which reviewed questions could be sent via e-mail to individual scientists. This collection of CGI scripts formed the basis of the *Moderator* package—the software developed to run the MAD Scientist Network site.

In short, the final plan for receiving and processing information went as follows:

1. A Web form asked for the person's name and grade level, the primary area of science represented by the question, the user's question, and any further comments. Only the question and area of science were required. Students lacking e-mail addresses could still ask questions anonymously and receive an answer by referring back to the Web site. Questions submitted through this form were converted to HTML documents by a CGI script. During this process an ID was assigned to each question to assist in the tracking of files.

2. After receipt, the question awaited review by a MadSci moderator. Moderators logged into a Web-CGI interface to review incoming questions and answers. The interface allowed moderators to respond to questions directly (refer people to other Web sites, etc.) or to select a scientist to answer the question. Questions were sent by e-mail to the selected scientist.

3. The scientist would then upload the answer through an online answer interface. As with questions, incoming answers were also formatted with HTML.

4. The moderators would review the answer for content and accuracy. If the answer passed review it would be posted to the Current Queue on the Web site; a carbon copy of the answer was sent to the person who asked the question if an address was provided.

5. Additional CGI scripts provided indexing and search functions so that any visitor to the site could access accumulated question-answer information in the archive.

Once the CGI interfaces had been adequately tested, the site officially went online. Fliers sent to the St. Louis public schools announced the service, as did presentations made by the YSP's Computer Literacy Team. Nonetheless, within a month, more than 99% of all questions came from outside of the St. Louis metropolitan area. In fact, roughly 20% came from overseas! A number of recommendations were made by the initial users of the MAD Scientist Network. Our ability to respond to and incorporate these suggestions allowed our site to develop into the service it has become.

Firstly, we received many requests from scientists at other institutions who were interested in answering questions. As volunteer sign up and question answering took place online, it took minimal effort to adapt our interfaces for use by scientists from around the world.

Secondly, the "other" category, originally designed to hold questions in biology and chemistry not covered by the defined areas, rapidly filled with questions concerning astronomy, physics, earth sciences, and other topics. Rather than turn these questions away, we expanded our recruitment of experts by posting messages to Usenet science groups, as well as local departments in St. Louis.

Over the next few years steady improvements in the *Moderator* interface created necessary functions. Some of these functions included the automatic tracking and "recycling" of unanswered questions and the keeping of "expert statistics" (i.e., information on experts) such as number of questions answered, outstanding questions, deferred questions, etc. to assist the moderators when selecting a scientist to receive a question.

The Web-based interface lies at the heart of the site. It distributes the review of hundreds of questions and answers among many individuals. It has permitted the expansion of our site from one that started with 40 experts and two moderators to one that has more than 600 scientists and 20 moderators. This expansion has been necessary to keep astride of exponential increases in traffic. The site averages over 50,000 visitors a month and receives one to two thousand questions during this same period. Current efforts are directed towards means of checking incoming questions against existing answers in the archive and structured organization of "exemplary" answers in the archive into FAQs covering specific areas of interest.

Lynn Bry, M.D./Ph.D., *lynn@madsci.wustl.edu*, is administrator of the MAD Scientist Network, and a pathology resident at Brigham & Women's Hospital, Harvard University Medical School.

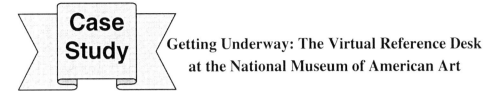

Getting Underway: The Virtual Reference Desk
at the National Museum of American Art

by Joan Stahl

Introduction

In 1993, when the National Museum of American Art launched its e-mail reference
service on America Online (AOL), "digital reference" was not a term in wide usage. Staff
alternately and awkwardly referred to the outreach initiative as "online reference,"
"virtual reference," and "e-mail reference" (the most accurate, but not the catchiest
appellation). The service was considered so unlike traditional reference that the
museum's library staff wanted no part of it; in fact, I embarked on the project alone with
support from the museum's administration. Today, the environment has vastly changed.
Many librarians around the country have taken their cue from the growth of AskA
services and are offering digital reference service in conjunction with traditional
reference. But the waters are still largely uncharted, and we can learn from one another as
we initiate and develop our programs. With the clarity that hindsight affords, I can share
some brief history of the National Museum of American Art's service and offer
suggestions for planning similar services.

History

The Smithsonian Institution was approached by AOL to become one of its small but
growing number of partners. The arrangement seemed a win-win situation. The
Smithsonian Institution was free to provide whatever information we wanted, and our
museums were the first represented on AOL. The Smithsonian Institution is a large
museum complex, and much of its operations are decentralized. Accordingly, the
participation in AOL was entirely voluntary for each museum.

The National Museum of American Art was the first museum to participate; this seemed
wholly appropriate, because the museum was at the forefront of the Smithsonian
Institution's experimentation with new technology. Although the museum has a national
mission, it has nevertheless long operated as a local Washington museum. The director
and staff were interested in exploring ways to reach an audience outside our region. Our
decision to start an area on AOL should not be interpreted as a way to exclude any
portion of the electronic community; quite the contrary, it has always been the museum's
intention to reach the widest audience possible. We began with AOL for a few reasons:
AOL was local, the arrangement required no initial outlay of funds for either staff or

67

equipment, and the museum had not yet developed its own Web site. In short, the opportunity presented itself. The interactive features at the museum site on AOL included online chats, message boards, entertaining contests, suggestion boxes, and a digital reference service.

In the spring of 1997, the digital reference service was made available at the museum's Web site independent of the AOL site (*http://nmaa-ryder.si.edu/referencedesk/*). This allowed us to extend the service to a larger audience. More recently, the museum disbanded its site on AOL, while retaining a link from AOL to the museum's service through AOL's Reference and Learn channel.

Mission

The service began quite simply. I managed the service by myself and incorporated the additional duties into my responsibilities as coordinator of the museum's Image Collection, which included overseeing our rather sizable slide and photo archive. I was happy to undertake the experiment because it provided me with the opportunity to keep abreast of emerging electronic resources and technologies. At the time, I knew of no other such service with a national constituency, and I wondered why librarians had quickly embraced document delivery and electronic reserves but were reluctant to advertise corresponding electronic reference services. My aims or ground rules were uncomplicated and few:

1. **Increase and diffuse art information to a national audience.** New technologies were exploding, and the Internet was full of vast and competing resources vying for users' time and money. Undoubtedly, the National Museum of American Art was better able than most other voices to provide information on American art.

2. **Provide answers whenever possible via e-mail.** While I referred patrons to useful resources, I also wanted to provide answers whenever possible. Art information is so difficult to access in many public libraries that have had budget cuts. The service gives patrons brief, useful information that is conveniently obtained and is communicated in a personalized manner. In most cases the response is a jumping-off point for further research on the part of the patron.

3. **Use institution resources to the fullest.** In addition to using the published resources available in the museum's outstanding library resources, I incorporated information from unique museum-developed resources including the Inventories of American Painting and Sculpture and curatorial files.

4. **Recruit new museum members.** The service could have a cost benefit to the museum in terms of increased membership.

Usage

At the start of the service, I received an average of 60 questions per month. That number rose quickly, peaking at 537 questions in February 1998; the average number of questions per month is now 350–450. Use is heaviest at peak times during the school year (September to November and February to April) with decreases during holidays and summer months. Users come from all 50 states as well as Latin and South America, Europe, Africa, and Asia. They range from elementary students to professionals in non-art fields to artists, those interested in the arts, graduate students in art history, and art professionals in museums and universities. The questions are the same as those that cross any reference desk but with a greater number of queries requesting electronic resources that can be remotely accessed. A small percentage of questions are "repeat questions"; this is not likely the case in other disciplines.

Lessons Learned (Planning for a New Service)

Nearly five years after the museum's reference service began, I can better assess what does and does not work and identify the essential ingredients for the implementation of a successful program. I have retrofitted the initiative of the National Museum of American Art's Reference Desk to work better for both staff and virtual visitors. As you contemplate the initiation of a similar service in your institution, consider the following suggestions presented in the form of questions:

1. Who is your audience and what is the scope of your service?

In other words, justify the purpose of the service. Is there a need for it? If yes, it is important to understand what information you can and cannot provide. Inevitably, you will receive questions "out of scope"; though they may be easy to answer, you cannot be all things to all users. Beyond that, you need to determine a reasonable turn around time for questions received.

The need for the Reference Desk at the National Museum of American Art is due to the nature of art books and their audiences. Art resources are expensive and serve a smaller audience than do resources in the sciences and social sciences. Consequently, most public libraries and many college and university libraries have limited collections, and virtual visitors are not always well-served when referred to such resources. Our statistics are ongoing testimony to the need for the Reference Desk, but the quantity of questions received is also the reason that we do not answer questions that fall outside the scope of the service. For those questions on African art or medieval art, for example, I send a polite reply such as:

> "I received your request on _____. You have wandered astray. The online reference service of the National Museum of American Art is dedicated to answering questions about American visual art and artists. Questions on other subjects are outside the scope of the service."

In planning your service, it is helpful for both you and the patron to estimate the turn around time. To that end, the Reference Desk Web form has a drop-down window that the patron can mark, indicating that he or she needs the information in one week, two weeks, one month, or any time. We strive to respond within five working days but advise patrons that the response time may vary based upon the traffic and the difficulty of the question.

2. Does the digital reference service reflect a broader department or institutional mission?

If the service reflects a broader mission, it is likely that you will be more successful in garnering both financial and technical support for the operation. The Smithsonian Institution's mission is broadly stated—"to increase and diffuse knowledge." Digital reference services are easily reflected in this statement. My efforts are focused on creating linkages between the Reference Desk and the objectives of the museum. For instance, the service is limited to the subject of the museum's collection (American art), and the Reference Desk serves the same audience that the museum strives to capture (national and international). Over time, the museum's administration has embraced the Reference Desk because it sees that the service carries out many of the museum's objectives.

3. Have you identified staffing needs and a reference model?

A one-person service has some appeal because you can oversee all aspects of the program. But is it practical? If not, how can you distribute queries and to whom? Is there a model of reference service that correlates with the service you want to deliver?

Over time, I have come to understand that a one-person service is impractical and difficult to maintain. But I am still trying to determine an acceptable and fundable way to distribute questions both inside and outside the institution.

4. What is your funding plan?

Digital reference does not pay for itself unless it is a fee-based service. If your service is not fee-based, how will you pay salaries and purchase equipment? Can you work with a development officer, contract out for such services, or undertake development yourself along with other responsibilities?

I have no magic answers. Based upon my experiences, as the service is more heavily used, funding issues will surface (due to increased staff, technology upgrades, etc.). At the National Museum of American Art, we are undertaking fund-raising initiatives to supplement the museum's support.

5. What is your marketing plan?

If you are making the effort to develop a digital reference service, do not overlook the need to advertise it. Consider appropriate places to advertise, based upon the profiles of your anticipated audience. I have often been asked why the Reference Desk retains a link from AOL to the museum's Reference Desk on the Web. From a marketing standpoint, the reason is obvious: AOL is the country's largest Internet provider, and many of its subscribers do not have other modes of access to the Web.

Marketing considerations will cover a range of possibilities including

- Placement of the service on your Web site (top level or buried several levels down)
- Advertising in institutional newsletters or publications
- Links on other Web sites that share subject interests
- Fliers and handouts.

The possibilities are limited only by your time and creativity.

6. What equipment and technical support are needed to operate the service, and are they accessible to you?

Digital reference is a technology-reliant service. It is critical that you have hardware and software to support the operational activities that are components of the service. The service you develop may require software customization and will certainly require technical support in the face of system problems. Is such support available in your institution, or do you need to contract for it?

Technical support is an issue for the Reference Desk; the service has outgrown its simple organization. It now requires support from the museum's Office of Information Technology, which is already pulled in several directions. With better planning, I might have been able to better prepare for the technical challenges the Reference Desk is now facing.

7. Who will train staff and what training is necessary?

If the questions are to be distributed, or if the service continues after you leave your present position, it is useful to identify staff training needs. A procedures manual may be time-consuming to create but will be well-utilized as your service grows. Additionally, you may want to create

- Boilerplate statements that cover repeat questions and situations (In the case of the Reference Desk, for example, I have statements about locating an appraiser and searching auction records.)
- Lists of useful Web sites
- Sample responses (to illustrate the opening, body, and closing of the response).

Conclusion

Digital reference makes sense. Information overload is a fact of life, and despite, or maybe because, so much information is accessible electronically, the average user often needs a human interface (a librarian or information specialist) to assist in navigating his or her way to appropriate resources. If you start a digital reference service, be assured users will come. It is easy to be overwhelmed by success and in short order find yourself unable to deliver the service you advertise due to the quantity of questions received. To avoid that situation, be realistic and plan.

Joan Stahl, *jstahl@nmaa.si.edu*, is the Coordinator of Image Collections for the National Museum of American Art, the Smithsonian Institution.

Module 2 Summary

This module provided background and techniques for creating a plan for new AskA services based on organization goals, a generalized service structure, and the experiences of existing AskA services.

- The AskA Plan is a document that outlines the potential components of a particular AskA service.

    1. Service goals should reflect goals of supporting organization(s) and should consider issues regarding potential audience, benefits of service to stakeholders, staff, users, etc.

    2. Organizations can benefit from supporting digital reference service in several ways including providing a method for collecting feedback from users and stakeholders; promoting national educational initiatives; and impacting education.

- All AskA services can be described in terms of a conceptual framework with three main components: methods for obtaining information on the environment (detectors); processes for building and providing service (rules), including resources for carrying out rules; and ultimate services provided (effectors).

- Organizations can create and implement their own AskA plan based on the general structure.

- Examples and experiences of exemplary AskA services can offer guidance and ideas in planning new services.

Module 3

Informing
Planning
Training
Prototyping
Contributing
Evaluating

Training

Training AskA Service Staff

Module Profile

This module is designed to assist organizations in planning, delivering, implementing, and managing training programs for AskA service staff and information specialists. Topics covered include the importance of training staff of AskA services and methods for creating a training plan, producing the training materials and delivery tools, and implementing and managing the overall training program. This module is divided into three main sections to accommodate organizations at different stages in training development: creating the training plan, producing the training program, and implementing and managing the training program. The three sections are preceded by an introduction to AskA training. At the conclusion of this module, you will be able to achieve the following goal:

Goal	Plan, produce, implement, and manage training programs for service staff and information specialists.
Prerequisites	Before participating in this module, you should be able to 1. Collect information on the general digital reference field and existing AskA services (see Module 1: Informing). 2. Determine the best way to build and maintain digital reference service within the organization (see Module 2: Planning), including human resources, policies, and procedures.
Objectives	At the completion of this module, you will be able to achieve the following objectives: 1. Understand the importance and purpose of planning an effective training program. 2. Identify staff members within the service who require training. 3. State three general phases involved in creating a training program for AskA service staff. 4. Create a plan for an AskA service's training program. 5. Produce the training program by creating materials, preparing delivery tools, and pilot testing materials and activities. 6. Implement training program according to planned schedule. 7. Manage training program by ongoing evaluation and revision.

75

3.1 Introduction to AskA Service Training

In a digital reference setting, *training* refers to the planned preparation of individuals involved in the creation, maintenance, and operations of a particular AskA service. As explained in the Introduction, this Starter Kit is intended as a set of self-instructional modules for AskA service administrators—those involved in the creation and maintenance of an AskA service. In this way, the Starter Kit as a whole serves as the main training component for AskA service administrators.

This module focuses on the steps necessary for planning training programs for those involved in AskA services on an operational level: information specialists (those responding to user questions) and support staff (those involved in operations other than or in addition to question answering). The steps presented in this module are based on the process of instructional design—a systematic approach to planning learner-focused instruction (Dick & Carey, 1996; Gustafson & Branch, 1997)—and experiences of existing AskA services.

Importance of Training

Effective training programs for AskA services are important for many reasons. The digital reference field involves innovative uses of technology, new aspects of reference and educational service (i.e., virtual vs. face-to-face), and other situations that demand a special set of skills. In addition, each AskA service has its own distinct policies and procedures that are to be followed by all staff and information specialists. Finally, AskA services rely on well-packaged, reproducible training programs and materials in order to accommodate the constant increase in numbers of information specialists and staff members as the service grows.

Who Is Trained?

The main audiences for training in an AskA service are information specialists and the staff who facilitate the work of information specialists and the overall service. (See Figure 3-1 for training functions by audience. Items in bold indicate areas targeted by individual AskA service training programs.)

Management
Instruction and resources on creating and maintaining digital reference services (e.g., *AskA Starter Kit*).

Information Specialists	**Support Staff**
Training on general issues in responding to digital reference queries **Service training on q/a procedures**	**Service training on day-to-day operations**

Figure 3-1: Training Solutions for AskA Service Staff

Different training programs are required to prepare each audience for its role as outlined below.

Training Information Specialists

AskA services generally place their largest training efforts on the individuals who respond to user inquiries. The main reason for this emphasis is that information specialists have the most direct interaction with users. The success of a digital reference service highly depends upon the effective interactions between information specialists and service users. Also, information specialists often make up a greater number and a more geographically diverse group of people than those in other staff roles do; therefore, more attention to logistical training needs is required.

Depending on a service's situation and available resources, training information specialists for digital reference service frequently consists of familiarizing information specialists with service policies and question answering procedures, sometimes allowing opportunities to practice responding to inquiries. Training may also include instructing information specialists to answer reference questions in general and to communicate effectively using the Internet.[16]

Implementation of training for information specialists varies from service to service. Some offer formal programs via distance or face-to-face, while others simply provide written resources (e.g., manuals) for information specialists to review before and during participation. See "Select Delivery Methods" and "Sample AskA Training Models" for examples of various types of training programs.

---

[16] For more general issues, refer to Kasowitz (1998).

77

Training Support Staff

Individuals who conduct day-to-day operations of a service may require training in service policy and procedure as well as use of resources and technology necessary for accomplishing given tasks (e.g., question routing, monitoring information specialists' responses, Web site development and maintenance, etc.).

Support staff may be further divided into different job positions and tasks (e.g., mentors/team leaders/administrators, technical support, etc.), each requiring slightly different training programs. This module highlights support staff as one group, although services will make training decisions based on individual situations.

Training programs for staff may include a written manual with service policies and procedures and specific job roles; some may involve participation in the question-answer training designed for information specialists as a way of becoming familiar with those operations. Training programs for support staff are often less formal than those for information specialists.

Who Plans, Produces, Delivers, and Manages Training Programs?

As will be discussed further in this module, the overall AskA training process can be broken into distinct phases requiring the expertise and efforts of different people. The planning of overall training programs and the development of activities and materials is often carried out by service administrators; however, these tasks can also be performed in conjunction with outside instructional design or training consultants. The implementation of training programs—which can involve delivering face-to-face sessions, electronically distributing materials, providing feedback on practice activities, etc.—can be conducted by service administrators, designated staff members, or information specialists who have demonstrated quality work and responsibility.

Phases in Building an AskA Service Training Program

There are a lot of issues to consider when creating any kind of training program from start to finish. This module breaks down the overall process into three separate phases based on principles of instructional design. AskA service administrators can follow these steps to create the most effective and efficient training programs for their AskA services:

1. Creating the Training Plan
2. Producing the Training Program
3. Implementing and Managing the Training Program

The three phases are further broken down by specific activities and questions conducted within each phase:

1. Creating the Training Plan (see Module 3.2)
    *   Establish training goals—What should information specialists and support staff be able to perform as a result of training?

    *   Select and organize training components—How should information be presented and training activities be administered in order to get the most out of the training program?

    *   Select delivery methods—What types of media and telecommunications tools should be used to deliver information and conduct training activities?

    *   Create a learner-assessment plan—What criteria will be used to determine whether or not trainees are prepared to perform required tasks following the training program?

2. Producing the Training Program (see Module 3.3)
    *   Create training materials—What are the most efficient and effective ways to develop and organize planned materials and activities?

    *   Prepare delivery tools—What is involved in securing and preparing tools and equipment to implement program?

    *   Pilot test—How will the program be tested in order to determine if training materials and activities will be successful?

3. Implementing and Managing the Training Program (see Module 3.4)

- <u>Schedule training events</u>—What are the best ways for managing the overall training program effectively and efficiently?

- <u>Provide feedback to trainees and staff</u>—What are the most efficient and effective ways to communicate feedback to help trainees and staff improve performance and stay motivated?

- <u>Evaluate and revise the program</u>—What efforts will be taken to evaluate the training program on an ongoing basis (e.g., instruments, analysis, revision)?

Each of the three phases will be discussed in detail in this module. The planning phase section contains the most information and examples since the results of planning set the stage for the following phases. The sections on the producing and the implementing and managing phases illustrate ways to put the training plan into action. Specific recommendations and examples from training programs will be presented in each section to help administrators plan and implement the most appropriate training programs for their AskA services. Although the phases are discussed separately and in a distinct order, it is expected that one will travel between stages throughout the process as appropriate.

Module 3.1 Summary
This section provided an introduction to training of AskA service staff.

- Training programs for AskA services help staff prepare for special situations involved in digital reference and understand and carry out service policy and procedures.

- Training programs for AskA services should be reproducible and accessible in order to accommodate the constant need for training new staff.

- The main audiences for training in an AskA service are information specialists and support staff who facilitate the work of information specialists. (This latter group may be further broken down depending on specific service roles.)

- The planning of training programs may be carried out by AskA service administrators, perhaps in conjunction with instructional design consultants; production, delivery, and management of training programs can be carried out by many different people including service administrators, designated staff members, or information specialists who have successfully completed training activities.

- The three main phases for building a training program are creating the training plan, producing the training program, and implementing and managing the training program. The phases are often conducted in a nonlinear manner.

3.2 Creating the Training Plan

This section describes the first phase of the overall process for creating a training program for AskA service staff: planning digital reference training programs for information specialists and support staff. The two main training audiences will be treated as separate entities although some issues may be the same for both. Also keep in mind that support staff will include one or more distinct positions depending on the service and thus may require more than one type of training program.

Establish Training Goals

Before thinking about glossy manuals or Internet-based interactive training sessions, it is important to focus on *what* the training audience must learn in order to carry out responsibilities. This step should occur at the beginning of the planning process because all other decisions will be based upon the information collected at this time, including current skill level of information specialists and support staff and the tasks they will be expected to perform.

This step involves four major activities as represented by the following questions:

1. What tasks will information specialists and support staff need to perform in order to carry out responsibilities?
2. What skills are required of information specialists and support staff in order to perform identified tasks?
3. To what extent are information specialists and support staff prepared to perform required tasks?
4. What will the training program attempt to accomplish in terms of preparing information specialists and support staff to perform required tasks?

The above questions can be answered by survey, observation, and analysis as described further.

1. What tasks will information specialists and support staff need to perform in order to carry out responsibilities?

The tasks to be performed by information specialists and support staff will be determined mostly from job descriptions already identified (according to the original AskA plan), but a more formal analysis may be taken to map out skills on a detailed level. Each audience (within the categories of information specialists and support staff) should be analyzed separately to find distinct tasks, although it is common for some to overlap.

For example, the primary task of an information specialist may be to answer questions about the subject of specialty (science, math, etc.) using expert knowledge. But what other steps are involved in answering questions?

- Are questions sent to the information specialist's personal e-mail account from a central account, or does the information specialist need to retrieve the inquiry message from a central location (e.g., Web-based system)?

- Does the response message need to include certain components (e.g., reference to resources, greeting to user, statement from service)?

- Are there any specific software or Internet functions that must be performed (e.g., Web searching, use of e-mail package)?

- What should information specialists do with the response after it is written (e.g., send it directly to the user, post it on a Web site, etc.)?

- What actions should information specialists take when a problem occurs (e.g., incorrect user address, unable to complete response within required time limit)?

If not previously answered, these questions should be examined now. One way to ensure that all steps are considered is to complete the task yourself or observe someone else completing the task. Make note of every step taken to get from the beginning to the end. Afterward, create a chart or list of all of the steps.

Figure 3-2 shows a sample task analysis in chart form adapted from an existing AskA service.

82

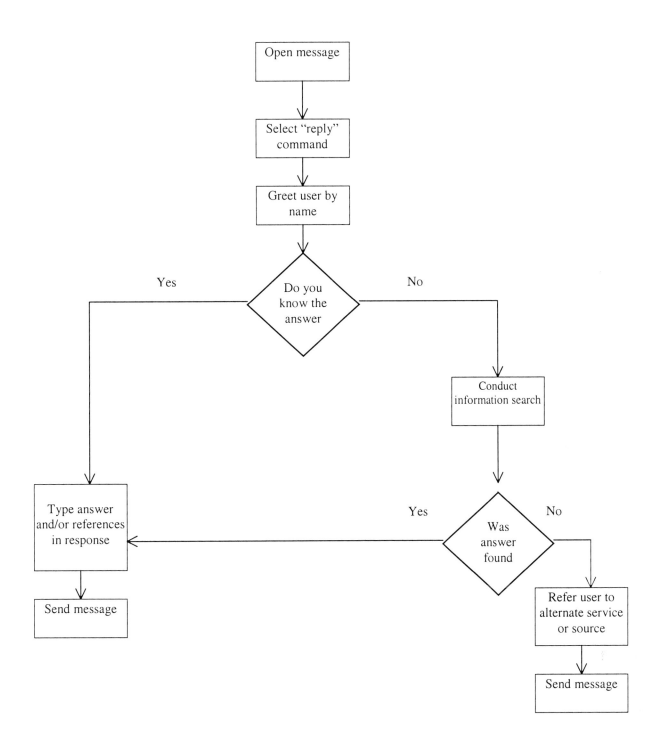

Figure 3-2: Task Analysis of Question/Answer Procedure for AskA Service
(Read from top to bottom)

*2. What skills are required of information specialists and support staff in order to
perform identified tasks?*

After the specific tasks are examined, it is possible to identify the skills necessary to
complete each task (see Table 3-1). Some skills will be considered **prerequisites**,
meaning they will not be covered in the formal training program; information specialists
or support staff are expected to have these skills before participating in the service. Those
not identified as prerequisites are areas that ought to be covered in the training program
in some way, either as major topics of instruction or supplemental information. (Specific
methods for covering such areas will be addressed later.)

Prerequisites will be determined mainly by survey of users (see question 3 below) but
also by service requirements and limitations. Prerequisites must be stated upfront as
requirements for participation.

Aside from required skills, information specialists and support staff are expected to have
certain technical capabilities in order to participate in the service. This may include
regular access to a personal e-mail account, Web browser, or word processing program,
and the ability to use more than one application at a time. It is important to distinguish
between necessary capabilities and those capabilities that would facilitate completion of
tasks. (For instance, in some cases it may be helpful to have access to both e-mail and a
Web browser at the same time for question answering, although it may not be required.)
These capabilities should also be stated as requirements for participation.

*3. To what extent are information specialists and support staff prepared to perform
required tasks?*

Once the specific tasks are identified, it is necessary to determine how well the training
audience is currently prepared to perform them. According to the specific tasks and
service policies and procedures, the following information may be sought:

What (and to what extent) do potential information specialists and support staff already
know about

- The subject or topic in which the service specializes?
- The user audience?
- Using necessary Internet tools and functions: Web browser, e-mail, Web design?
- Using specific software applications or functions?

- Identifying and locating information resources (and information within resources) to support responses?
- Communicating effectively and appropriately using the Internet?
- Providing feedback on information specialists' responses? (for support staff).

Answers to some of these questions will clarify any assumptions made about what the audience currently knows before training (prerequisites) and consequently provides information on what should be included in training.

This type of information can be gathered through standard survey mechanisms such as written questionnaires, interviews, focus groups, etc. with potential information specialists and support staff. Perhaps the easiest, quickest method of collecting this information is a questionnaire distributed via e-mail or on a Web form. See Figure 3-3, "Pre-Training Questionnaire for New Experts."

People to target include those who have already expressed interest in participating in the service and people who you would expect to have similar background knowledge to potential service staff (e.g., high school English teachers for a literature-related AskA service). Methods for recruiting individuals to respond to survey questions may include posting requests on a Web site or on e-mail discussion lists.

Figure 3-3 Pre-Training Questionnaire for New Experts

Please check the most appropriate answer so we can make our training program right for you!

1. How many years have you been working in this particular subject area?
   1-5   _____
   6-10   _____
   11-15   _____
   16 or more   _____

2. How often do you use e-mail?
   7 times a week or more   _____
   4 to 6 times a week   _____
   1 to 3 times a week   _____
   Less than once a week   _____
   Never   _____

3. What do you use e-mail for?
   Work   _____
   Listservs (Electronic discussion groups) _____
   Social correspondence   _____
   Other:_____

4. Where is your Internet connection? (Check all that apply)
   Home _____
   Work _____
   Other:_____

5. What type of WWW access do you have?
   Text only (Lynx)   _____
   Text and images   _____

6. What information resources are available to you?
   Internet   _____
   CDs   _____
   Online databases   _____
   Print resources   _____
   Other:_____

7. What skills would you like to acquire (or sharpen) in preparing to carry out your responsibilities as an "expert"?

8. What information would be helpful to you to know in preparing to carry out your responsibilities as an "expert"?

Table 3-1 contains a list of tasks with corresponding skills. The tasks included are adapted from a manual for information specialists of a subject-oriented AskA service (MAD Scientist Network, 1997a). Prerequisite skills are indicated by a check mark in the prerequisite column. Those skills that are expected to be covered in training are in bold type. Skills will be later translated into objectives and then met with specific training materials and activities.

Table 3-1: Tasks and Corresponding Skills for Question-Answer Procedure

Task	Skill	Prerequisite?
1. Open e-mail message.	1. Proficiency with personal e-mail program	√
2. Choose "respond" command **or** open new file in word processing program.	2. Proficiency with personal e-mail program or proficiency with word processing program	√ √
3. Greet user by name.	**3. Knowledge of service question-answer policy and procedure**	
4. Provide factual answer.	4a. Subject expertise	√
	4b. Ability to communicate effectively via Internet	
	4c. Familiarity with user audience (K–12 students)	
5. Provide references to additional resources on topic.	**5a. Knowledge of overall reference process**	
	5b. Use of periodical indexes	√
	5c. Use of library or collection catalog	√
	5d. Web-searching skills	
	5e. Knowledge of HTML (to include links)	
6. Sign name at end of message.	**6. Knowledge of service question-answer policy and procedure**	
7. Resolve problems during question-answer process.	**7. Knowledge of service question-answer policy and procedure**	
8. Paste response into online message form OR send e-mail response to Web site administrator.	8a. Proficiency with Web browser and word processing functions for copy and paste	√
	8b. Ability to open more than one application at once (optional)	
	8c. Proficiency with personal e-mail program	√

Work Sheet 3-1: Task and Skill Table

Task	Skill	Prerequisite?

The case study "Electronic Reference Service Issues and Necessary Skills" describes necessary skills for particular situations involved in the question-answer process from the perspective of one public library electronic reference service.

4. What will the training program attempt to accomplish in terms of preparing information specialists and support staff to perform required tasks?

After identifying what the training audience must know and what the audience currently knows, you can determine where the training efforts should focus. Building on the analysis represented in Table 3-1, it is possible to create a goal statement to define what the training program will try to accomplish (in terms of trainee performance). From this statement, you can later create specific objectives to guide the content of your training programs. Documentation of this type is not only helpful in guiding pre-training activities but also aids in justifying training efforts to organizations supporting the service.

Below are examples of training goals for information specialists and support staff:

Information Specialists Goal
> Information specialists will respond to user inquiries using appropriate information resources and individual subject expertise.

Support Staff Goal
> Service moderators will support the work of information specialists by reviewing and organizing incoming questions; managing, reviewing, and revising information specialists' responses; and providing feedback to information specialists regarding responses.

Select and Organize Training Components

This stage offers opportunities to map out the information, ideas, and activities to include in a training program. Also at this time, many decisions are made regarding how training materials will be developed and organized. Some questions answered during this stage include the following:

1. What skills must the training audience have in order to achieve the ultimate goal?
2. How should necessary information and ideas be communicated to the training audience?

1. What skills must the training audience have in order to achieve the ultimate goal?

In order to achieve the previously identified goals, information specialists and support staff members will demonstrate a variety of other skills identified during the task analysis. These skills are planned out in the form of **objectives**. Some objectives refer to ultimate goals while others indicate steps necessary to reach those goals. Objectives not only set out what the information specialists and support staff should do after training, but will help guide the administrator or instructional designer in presenting content.

Below are some sample objectives for information specialists who refer users to information resources:

1. Prepare a response to a user inquiry by opening message in personal e-mail account, selecting "reply" and "include original message" options, placing user address in reply line and service address in the cc line, and greeting user by name.

2. Research user's question by searching the Internet and other print and electronic sources.

3. Respond to user's question by typing or electronically transferring information from the original source to the reply message.

4. Conclude response by referring user to additional sources, signing name, and sending message.

5. Resolve problematic situations during response process according to service guidelines.

Information specialists who are required to use their own subject knowledge rather than information sources may have a different set of objectives including these:

1. Acknowledge user's previous efforts in answering question.

2. State concepts in age-appropriate language.

3. Allow the user opportunities to answer similar questions on his or her own by providing sample questions, suggesting additional activities, or both.[17]

---

[17] This example was adapted from Ask Dr. Math's *Guide to Writing Responses,* 1998 *http://forum.swarthmore.edu/dr.math/guide/*.

Support staff may be required to perform a variety of tasks such as the following:

1. Use central system to review and route incoming questions to appropriate information specialists.
2. Review information specialists' responses according to set of criteria outlined in service guidelines for responding to inquiries.
3. Provide feedback to information specialists using appropriate language and tone.
4. Locate Internet and other sources to include as references (supplemental information) in previously written responses.

Once the goals and objectives are set, it is easier to see where to concentrate the training efforts. The following sections will illustrate how training components are selected with help from the objectives.

2. How should necessary information and ideas be communicated to the training audience?

For each objective identified, choose the most appropriate **treatment:** the content and the activity or materials to communicate the content. For instance, if an objective states that information specialists are expected to respond to user inquiries by following certain procedures, an appropriate treatment may be to provide opportunities for the trainee to compose practice responses.

Objectives that imply general skills—such as Internet searching, information skills, electronic communication skills, etc.—are addressed in a document created by the Virtual Reference Desk project. *Guidelines for Information Specialists of K–12 Digital Reference Services* (Kasowitz, 1998) can be used in conjunction with training provided by individual services. It offers general tips and suggestions for providing information to K–12 community members over the Internet using an information problem-solving approach (a method for addressing questions by applying critical-thinking skills and assessing information resources).

Choose and Organize Content. The first step in selecting content should be to analyze the objectives established from service requirements and audience characteristics. For instance, if an objective states that information specialists should refer users to Web sites as part of the response message, it may be necessary to offer some guidance on how to search for and evaluate Web sites (this is assuming that a certain number of trainees are not already proficient in this area). See Table 3-2 for an example of the evolution of objectives into content and then possible treatments.

It is also helpful to consider common topic areas highlighted in AskA service training programs. From an initial analysis of training materials of exemplary AskA services, several areas have been identified (keep in mind that many areas come directly from individual service policies and procedures). (See Table 3-2 for these common areas and related contents included in services' training materials.)

Table 3-2: Common Content Areas in AskA Training Materials

Type of Staff	Areas	Content Examples
All	General information and background about service	• Functions and individuals involved • Contact information • Sponsoring or supporting organizations • Service mission, goals, and objectives • History of service
All	Description of job role	• Responsibilities/expectations • Required skills • Required technical capabilities

All/
Information Specialists (IS)
	Question-answer procedure	Instructions for
		• Receiving or claiming questions
		• Researching question (reference process)
		• Writing responses
		  ◊ Required components
		  ◊ General approach and tone
		  ◊ Suggested format
		• Sending response
		  ◊ Time limit
		  ◊ What happens to response
		• Technology and interfaces used in q-a

Support staff	Procedures for routing questions and evaluating responses	• Criteria for evaluating IS responses • Suggestions for providing feedback • Technology used
All	Problem-solving/Troubleshooting	Instructions for handling situations such as: • IS can't answer question within time limit • IS can't find answer • User question is unclear, inappropriate, etc.
All	Exemplary responses	Include examples • Within text to illustrate points • As separate section or resource

All	Role or use of supporting resources in answering questions	• State possible sources
		  ◊ Internal (indexes, archive, FAQs)
		  ◊ External sources (Web sites, texts)
		• Provide support for using the Web
		  ◊ Using search engines
		  ◊ Evaluating Web sites
		• Instructions for incorporating citations or sources within response
		  ◊ Linking to Web pages
		  ◊ Uploading files

Another possible area to consider is information or directions for updating, delivering, and managing the training program. This type of information in the form of a "trainer's manual" or "instructor's guide" would be useful for staff members involved in these functions, especially in situations where staff changes occur.

Choose Materials and Activities. Once you've identified the content to include in the training program, it's time to choose a format to communicate the information. The two general categories for formats are **materials** (e.g., handbooks, manuals, how-to lists) and **activities** (e.g., shadowing, practice questions with guided feedback, etc.). Specific media for presenting information and strategies used to carry out activities will be discussed in the following section, "Select Delivery Methods."

The following table (3-3) shows sample objectives and their corresponding treatments in terms of content as well as possible materials or activities. The table is intended as a general guide to present common objectives and treatments used in AskA service training programs. Keep in mind that individual services will require treatments that address objectives based on special responsibilities and skills such as specific question-answer procedures, software or Internet tools used to operate the service, information resources specific to the organization or content area, etc.

Table 3-3: Possible Treatments Based on Specific Objectives

Objective	Treatment	
	Content	**Materials/Activities**
1. Prepare a response to a user inquiry by opening user's message in personal e-mail account, selecting "reply" and "include original message" options, placing user address in reply line and service address in cc line, and greeting user by name.	• Service guidelines for responding to user inquiries • Steps for completing response • Instructions for using technology necessary to perform response • List of required response components • Examples of successful responses	• Policy and procedure manual • Checklist of steps for completing response • Checklist of required response components • Examples interspersed throughout manual • Practice questions and feedback on practice responses
2. Perform and promote information problem-solving process in responding to user questions.	• Steps in general information problem-solving process • Exemplary responses	• Resource on general digital reference skills (Kasowitz, 1998) • Section of manual with service-specific exemplary responses containing information problem-solving tips
3. Create clear and effective message using clear language and layout, using a friendly and appropriate tone, and motivating users to learn.	Criteria and examples for creating clear and effective messages	• Resource on general digital reference skills (Kasowitz, 1998) • Section of manual with service-specific examples of exemplary messages and poor quality messages (non-examples)

Work Sheet 3-2: Training Objectives and Solutions

Objective	Treatment	
	Content	Materials/Activities

Select Delivery Methods

During this step it is important to decide how the overall training program should be implemented to help the training audience achieve goals. This is the part that most people associate with a particular training program—the actual products and events. What will the whole training package consist of when it is complete? From the situation in the previous table, we may envision the following two training scenarios (see "Sample AskA Training Models" for additional examples):

Scenario One
1. Participants are directed to a Web-based policy and procedure manual with checklists to be printed out, exemplary responses, and reference to the VRD Guidelines document on the Web (Kasowitz, 1998).

2. Administrator e-mails practice questions to each training participant once the participant has reviewed the materials.

3. Training participants respond to practice questions and return responses to administrator for review and feedback.

Scenario Two
1. Service coordinator distributes to each participant in a face-to-face session print-based policy and procedure manual with checklists and pointers to VRD Guidelines document on the Web (Kasowitz, 1998).

2. Each participant observes current information specialists performing task of responding to user question.

3. Participants claim practice questions from Web site.

4. Each participant returns practice response to trainer (a current information specialist) for review; feedback is delivered electronically and face-to-face.

Clearly the main difference between the two scenarios is that the first scenario delivers training entirely from a distance, while the second scenario involves some face-to-face interaction and direct observation. Since many services' staff members are widely distributed geographically and all AskA services use electronic communication in daily activities, most services employ some type of "distance training."[18] For example, training manuals are accessible on the Web, and practice activities involve using the same e-mail or Web-based communications tools that will be used during service participation.

---

[18] For more information on distance education, see Kerka (1996) and Romiszowski (1993).

Each service should decide for itself how much of training to deliver electronically and when. The following issues can be considered in making this decision:

- Geographic location of training participants
- Access of participants to Internet: speed of connection, type of Web browser, e-mail program
- Resources of AskA service organization to develop and distribute electronic materials
- Participants' skill with necessary tools upon entrance to the training program.

The important thing to remember is that one training program can incorporate several different methods and tools (e.g., e-mail, Web page, group discussion) depending on the best way to communicate a certain idea, reinforce a concept, or improve and build a skill. This can include a combination of distance and face-to-face components.

Table 3-4 shows possible types of information and activities to be delivered as part of a training program and possible ways of communicating the information and carrying out activities. This is just a sample, but it includes Internet tools as well as print-based and face-to-face interventions. Also keep in mind that several different types of tools and approaches may be used to deliver a given set of information or carry out an activity, but some tools and approaches are more effective for a given set of trainees and situations.

Table 3-4: Possible Treatments and Delivery Tools Matrix

Delivery Tools	Present Information	Discussion	Practice	Feed-back	Job Aids[19]	Comments
Web page	X		X	X	X	<ul><li>Attractive presentation.</li><li>Allows hyperlinks to basic and supplemental information.</li><li>Authentic practice possible through Web forms.</li><li>Allows access to Web-based service resources (archive, question-answer distribution system).</li></ul>
E-mail	X	X	X	X	X	<ul><li>Limited formatting options due to need to accommodate UNIX-based systems.</li><li>Good for asynchronous communication and authentic practice if question-answer process is e-mail–based.</li></ul>
File transfer	X				X	<ul><li>Can allow sharing of different types of files, from simple text documents to files with graphics and video.</li><li>Files can be viewed using downloadable reader software such as Adobe Acrobat.</li><li>Files must be compatible with participants' systems.</li></ul>
Interactive communications environment (MOO, IRC)	X	X	X	X		<ul><li>Good for synchronous communication with several participants.</li><li>Sometimes difficult to manage for large groups.</li><li>Software must be compatible with participants' systems.</li></ul>

---

[19] Job aids are supplemental resources intended to help the trainee come up to speed during training and to provide support for performance on-the-job.

Delivery Tools	Present Information	Discussion	Practice	Feed-back	Job Aids[20]	Comments
Print-based materials	x		x		x	<ul><li>Good for face-to-face sessions.</li><li>Doesn't allow practice in authentic setting but can help sharpen some skills.</li><li>For distance training, copy and mail costs may exceed costs for creating and distributing electronic resources.</li></ul>
Instructor-led presentation	x	x			x hand-outs	<ul><li>Good for introducing topics; must follow up with review and practice and feedback.</li><li>Can be done at conferences, service site, etc.</li></ul>
Instructor-led class	x	x	x	x	x hand-outs	<ul><li>Works if participants and instructor are at same geographic location (e.g., university campus).</li><li>Can cover broader issues of digital reference (see AskA Training Model 5).</li><li>Practice is authentic only if trainees have access to necessary technology.</li></ul>
One-on-one mentoring	x	x	x	x	x	<ul><li>Allows attention to individual participants' needs and skills.</li><li>Works in face-to-face or distance situations along with print materials, electronic materials, or both.</li></ul>
Computer-based instruction	x		x	x	x	<ul><li>Encapsulated programs for individual instruction; practice is not authentic unless integrated with Web or e-mail component.</li><li>Development of product is time and cost intensive.</li></ul>

---

[20] Job aids are supplemental resources intended to help the trainee come up to speed during training and to provide support for performance on-the-job.

As previously mentioned, training programs can include a combination of different materials, activities, and delivery tools. Some possible combinations based on training programs of existing AskA services include the following (see "Sample AskA Training Models" for examples of each scenario):

1. **Text-Based Only (Responses Screened After Training).** Manuals or other materials are available online or distributed via e-mail to training participants. Performance of participants (e.g., question answering, question routing) is monitored after training, on the job. (*Sample AskA Training Model 1.*)

2. **Text—Practice—Feedback.** Manuals and other materials (e.g., job aids) are available to participants. Following an opportunity to read the materials, participants are directed to or receive practice activities (e.g., practice questions to which trainees are expected to respond according to training materials). Service administrator offers feedback on practice activity performance. Practice-feedback cycle is repeated until trainee performs task successfully and is ready to participate in the service. (*Sample AskA Training Model 2.*)

3. **Text—Shadow and Observation—Practice—Feedback.** Training participants are given general training materials and then are able to observe current staff performing job tasks. Training participant then responds to practice activities (i.e., practice questions) and receives feedback from current staff members until ready to participate. (*Sample AskA Training Model 3.*)

4. **In-Person Class—Text—Practice—Feedback.** A group of participants attend an organized class led either face-to-face or virtually (e.g., chat, video conferencing, Web, e-mail). Participants read training materials and then complete a series of practice activities and receive feedback from current staff members. (*Sample AskA Training Model 4.*)

Another mode of communication during training includes listserv discussions between participants and trainers. These discussions can be used to clarify areas of confusion and share specific information such as reminders, schedules, etc. Listserv discussions are also a good way to document important information about the training program itself, such as reactions of participants to certain activities and materials.

Create Learner Assessment Plan

During the planning phase it is important to decide how trainees will be assessed; in other words, how will you know when a training participant is ready to perform successfully as an information specialist or AskA staff member? This issue may be most prominent in training sessions for information specialists who are expected to perform the defined task of responding to user queries. Some services do not allow trainees to pass the training program until they demonstrate proficiency (e.g., they respond to practice questions successfully); others allow their information specialists to begin responding to queries right away, but the responses are monitored by other staff members. (Some service policies require that all outgoing responses be monitored, while some allow responses to bypass the screening process once the information specialist is deemed ready.)

Whatever type of assessment plan is selected, it is important to communicate to training participants the criteria and methods by which they will be judged. When assessing information specialists' responses to user queries, a number of different criteria may be used including the following:

- Inclusion of all response components
- Adherence to established turnaround time
- Use of appropriate tone and language
- Accuracy of facts and resources included
- Relevance to question
- Visual appeal
- Adherence to specific service policies.

In addition to judging trainees' performance for the sake of determining readiness for participation, it is important to communicate to trainees how well they are achieving goals and what they can do to improve. Some services use a structured grading scale to inform information specialists as to the quality of their responses; others provide open-ended feedback to trainees with constructive criticism and suggestions for improvement. See "Sample AskA Training Models" for examples of practice and feedback options. More detailed discussion on providing feedback is found in Module 3.4: Implementing and Managing.

Module 3.2 Summary

This section covers the steps and decisions necessary for creating a training plan.

- The planning phase is broken down into four main steps: establish training goals, select and organize training components, select delivery methods, and create a learner assessment plan.

- During the "establish training goals" step, you will do the following:
  1. Identify tasks and skills that are required for information specialists and staff to carry out responsibilities.
  2. Analyze trainees to determine how well information specialists and support staff are prepared to perform required tasks.
  3. Set training goals that outline what the training program will attempt to accomplish in terms of preparing information specialists and support staff to perform required tasks.

- During the "select and organize training components" step, you will do the following:
  1. Identify objectives that the training audience (information specialists, support staff, or both) need to perform in order to achieve the ultimate goal.
  2. Select a set of "treatments" (content, materials, and activities) that outline how information and ideas should be communicated to the training audience.

- During the "select delivery methods" step, you will do the following:
  1. Select the combination of products and events that make up the overall training program.
  2. Select tools to deliver training (e.g., communications technology, instructors, publishing environments, etc.)

- During the "create learner assessment plan" step, you will do the following:
  1. Identify criteria to measure how well learners achieved objectives.
  2. Identify methods to test learners and provide feedback.

3.3 Producing the Training Program

Once a training plan is established it is time to put the plan into action. At this point, you will have set goals for participants of the training program; selected objectives and the content, materials, and activities to help participants reach objectives; determined the training products and events and the tools to deliver training; and established a plan for evaluating training participants during and following training activities.

This section describes the second phase of the overall process for creating a training program for AskA service staff: producing the materials and activities for a training program, preparing for delivery, and testing the program to determine its effectiveness.

Create Training Materials

Depending on the training plan, specific materials may be created or compiled from an existing set of resources. For example, a service may create a handbook to guide the trainee through training activities and will refer to existing materials for support: question-answer policy and procedure manual, lists of helpful Web sites, etc.

There are some important issues to consider when creating any type of materials that are intended to be instructional in nature (i.e., intended to assist someone to learn new skills or knowledge). This section outlines the following issues and provides examples.

Set Expectations

State objectives of the training program clearly and early on in the program. (As previously discussed, it works best to use the objectives to guide the content of the overall program, so these ideas will be reinforced throughout.) Objectives can be presented in training materials in a variety of ways. The following example presents sample objectives for information specialists:

> When you finish this training session, you will be able to respond to an incoming user question by
>
> 1. Incorporating all required response components.
> 2. Using service resources and external Internet resources to research answers to user queries.
> 3. Using your own e-mail program to receive, compose, and send messages.

The following example presents sample objectives for support staff:

Following this training session, you will be able to

1. Use central system to review and route incoming questions to appropriate information specialists.

2. Review information specialists' responses according to set of criteria outlined in service guidelines for responding to inquiries.

3. Provide feedback to information specialists using appropriate language and tone.

4. Locate Internet and other sources to include as references (supplemental information) in previously written responses.

Create Positive Attitude

It is important that the tone of the overall training program be positive and motivating. Language should be friendly and light, and information should be clear and concise so that the overall training experience is as pleasant and time efficient as possible. Since many information specialists and support staff work as volunteers, it is also important to let staff know how much their efforts are appreciated.

Motivational components in training materials and communications can include these:

- Attention-getting language (humor, anecdotes, information phrased as questions)
- Visuals (graphics, illustrations, charts, bullet lists)
- Interactivity (space for notes in materials; opportunities for discussion on e-mail lists)
- Confidence-building language (e.g., "Don't worry if you have trouble searching the Web at first. It takes practice!")
- Acknowledgment of participants' busy schedules and professional expertise
- Description of rewards that staff can gain from participation in service:
  ◊   intrinsic (e.g., personal satisfaction, professional experience)
  ◊   extrinsic (e.g., information resource products, promotional items, salary, etc.)

Examples for creating a positive attitude during training include the following:

Thank you for participating in Ask An Engineer! As professional engineers, you bring your talents and expertise to this special program. Your volunteered time and services are appreciated!

Following this training session you will join the other members of the Ask A Librarian team in fulfilling personal and professional needs and gaining important reference and technology skills!

Provide Clear Information and Examples

State concepts clearly and use contexts that are familiar to the intended audience. Offer authentic, specific examples to illustrate concepts such as including required response components and providing feedback on information specialists' responses. Examples will not only help to illustrate important ideas but will help familiarize trainees with the types of situations they will face as information specialists or support staff. Examples for providing clear information and examples in training materials are below.

The following example illustrates a section from a manual for information specialists of an AskA service for K–12 students:

> In responding to student questions, stress the importance of using a variety of information sources. It is important to remind students that the Internet is not the only place to look for answers to their questions, and that they may have to consult a few different resources. For instance, an encyclopedia is sometimes the best and fastest source.
>
> > You might say something like this in your response:
> >
> > > . . . Although there are many Web sites about hurricanes, a simple article in a general or science encyclopedia will best answer your question: 'How are hurricanes formed?' Ask your school library media specialist to guide you to an encyclopedia or to other resources on hurricanes in your school library media center . . .

The next example illustrates a section from a manual for AskA service moderators that explains the process for screening incoming questions for distribution:

> In order for a question to be distributed to an information specialist for a response it must be
>
> • Comprehensible
> • Related to the subject of science
> • Unable to be answered by reviewing service resources
> • Unable to be answered by reviewing known Internet resources.
>
> For example, the question "What should I do for my science fair project?" should not be sent to an information specialist, because the student can find an answer by reviewing some of the sites recommended on the service's "Science Fair Link" page.[21]

---

[21] This example was adapted from the *MADSci Moderator's Manual*: *http://www.madsci.org/ask_expert/moderators.html*

Provide Opportunities for Practice and Feedback

This is executed differently by different services. Many services extend practice and feedback past the training program by simply assessing staff performance on the job (e.g., information specialists' responses to user questions, etc.); in fact, some services conduct practice and feedback *only* after training (see "Sample AskA Training Models").

It is advantageous to incorporate a practice and feedback component in AskA training programs for several reasons including these:

- Participant performance indicates whether or not they are ready to perform their new roles and tasks successfully.
- Feedback from service administrators or trainers informs trainees of ways to improve their work (e.g., responses to service users).
- Results from practice activities serve to judge the effectiveness of the training program (e.g., if all participants struggle with a certain task during a practice activity, it may be necessary to present the particular information in a different way).

See Module 3.4 for tips on providing feedback to training participants.

The following example includes a description of practice activities from an online training manual for information specialists of an AskA service for K–12 students:

> Once you've reviewed this training manual, you are ready to practice responding to some sample student questions. When you are ready to receive your first practice question, please complete and submit the form below. Your second practice question will be sent to you after you receive feedback on your first response. This process will continue until you and your trainer feel that you are ready to join an existing volunteer team.

The next example includes a training agenda for in-house staff of information specialists (System-wide guide to AskERIC question answering, 1998).

> - Review training manual.
> - "Shadow" veteran information specialists to observe searching methods and response preparation.
> - Complete exercises to practice using e-mail program and Internet browser.
> - Begin trial period where responses to user inquiries will be monitored and feedback will be offered on content, format, and tone.

See "Sample AskA Training Models" for more examples of practice and feedback activities for AskA training programs.

Provide Post-Training Help and Reinforcement

Some training participants may find it difficult to remember all of the important information presented during training. It is a good idea to provide "job aids"—handy reminders of how to perform tasks and supplemental resources that participants can refer to after the training program. Examples of job aids may include the following:

- Checklists
- Diagrams
- Lists of additional resources (Web links, bibliographies)
- Directions for using required tools (e.g., databases, question-routing software)
- Exemplary work (or non-examples).

In addition to resource-based job aids, services may offer access to staff members who can serve as mentors to new participants following the training session. This type of arrangement allows new staff members to ease into their roles by relying on support from those who are more familiar with the process.

The following example includes a checklist of response components as one job aid:

> Here is the list of components to include when writing responses to users:
>
> 1. Include original message.
> 2. Greet user by name.
> 3. Short factual response (if appropriate).
> 4. Reference to resources used to answer question.
> 5. Directions for finding resources.
> 6. Name of information specialist.

The following example lists supplemental resources for learning to use search engines:

> Below are some good resources to help you choose the best Internet search tools for particular situations:
>
> Sink or Swim: Internet Search Tools & Techniques by Ross Tyner, M.L.S., Okanagan University College
> *http://oksw01.okanagan.bc.ca/libr/connect96/search.htm*
>
> Understanding WWW Search tools *http://www.indiana.edu/~librcsd/search/*
>
> Web Searching Guide from the Internet Public Library
> *http://ipl.sils.umich.edu/ref/Websearching.html*
>
> SCOTT *http://www.askscott.com/*

Prepare Delivery Tools

Depending on the combination of delivery tools selected, preparation will consist of different types of actions and decisions. By this stage, delivery tools will have already been selected based on several issues including accessibility and skills of participants (see "Select Delivery Methods" in Module 3.2). At this stage, delivery tools are prepared for production and implementation of instructional materials and activities. For each type of delivery tool selected, it is important to consider the following issues:

Technical Issues for AskA Service and Participants

These can include development issues such as establishing Web space for an online training manual or implementation issues such as making sure a classroom is wired for Internet connection or that all participants' names are added to the electronic discussion list.

Skills Necessary for Individuals Developing, Implementing, and Managing Tools

It is a good idea to make sure that everyone involved in preparing and using selected delivery tools has the necessary expertise or can be trained in the required areas. This can include basic writing skills, proficiency with Web site design (e.g., HTML, Web editing software, graphics design, etc.), or experience in listserv management.

Aesthetic Possibilities and Limitations of Tool(s)

Some tools allow more flexibility in design than others. Training materials intended for e-mail distribution on UNIX-based systems should include only those formatting options available for text-only (or ASCII) documents. Therefore, more creativity is needed to make the document look visually appealing (e.g., adequate white space, borders with asterisk marks or dashes in between sections, etc.). Materials distributed on Web pages, however, may include brightly colored graphics, animation, and multiple font types.

See Table 3-5 for examples of issues to consider when preparing different types of delivery tools. This table does not represent a comprehensive list of issues.

Table 3-5 Issues in Preparing Delivery Tools

Delivery Tools	Technical Issues	Skills	Aesthetic Issues
Web page	Secure Web space	Knowledge of HTML or Web editing software	Balance of text, graphics, animation (depends on identified technical capabilities of participants)
E-mail	Collect participants' e-mail addresses	List management (knowledge of listserv or other discussion list software)	Must use creativity to present information for those participants using UNIX systems (white space, borders).
File transfer	Do administrators and participants have file transfer software? Which programs and versions are participants using?	Knowledge of file transfer software	Create documents according to capabilities of specific programs.
Interactive communications environment (MOO, IRC)	If text-based, users need access to UNIX server and directions for entering chat environment. If graphics-based (using specific software package such as The Palace (*http://www.palacespace.com/*), service staff must create training environment and users must have necessary software to participate as well as passwords and directions for entering environment.	Manage or guide chat discussions Create environment for graphical chat.	Text-based communications environments are limited in terms of design. Software for graphical communication allows wide selection of graphics, animation, sound, etc. in creating special environments.
Print-based materials	Copies; printing and binding; mailing and distributing	Writing and formatting	Balance of text and graphics
Instructor-led presentation or class	Check on availability of equipment (overhead or LCD projector), Internet connection, etc.; chairs, lighting, etc.	Presentation or teaching skills; use of presentation software; operation of equipment	Presentation software offers a variety of opportunities for graphic and text design.
One-on-one mentoring	If face-to-face, do both people require access to computer? Physical space for both people; establish participant-mentor partnerships	Interpersonal skills; ability to accommodate training delivery to individual needs.	

110

Pilot Test the Training Program

In order to determine whether or not the training materials and activities will be successful, it is helpful to conduct a first run of the training program on a pilot group. This works best when members of the pilot group intend to serve as staff for the service. The only difference between a pilot test and an actual training session is that the pilot test is used to pay special attention to the effectiveness and efficiency of training materials and events and learner performance. The point of the pilot tests is to catch any major flaws before final drafts of materials are produced or major decisions are made about tools and events. Results from pilot tests can save services money, time, and other resources. See Module 4 for issues in pilot testing the overall AskA service.

Questions asked during a training program pilot test may address the following topics:
- Effectiveness of materials
  ◊   clarity and comprehensibility of content
  ◊   visual appeal of materials
  ◊   helpfulness of practice activities
- Efficiency of overall session
  ◊   amount of time spent on training
  ◊   ability to use the technology necessary to participate in training (e-mail program, Web-based database, etc.)
- Extent to which trainees are prepared to perform staff duties

Questions are most effective when they are designed to elicit more than a "yes" or "no" response. For instance, you can include the following:

- Multiple-choice responses ("On a scale from 1 to 4 where 1 = 'not at all prepared' and 4 = 'very prepared,' please indicate how you feel about responding to user questions at this time.")
- Opportunities for open-ended responses ("What additional information do you think should be included in the training materials?")

During and after a pilot test, different evaluation methods can be used to determine results. Some services may distribute instruments such as questionnaires via e-mail or the Web (see Figure 3-4), while others may hold informal conversations on an e-mail discussion list.

Figure 3-4: Training Pilot Test Questionnaire Distributed Via E-mail

Information Specialist Training Session 1
Questionnaire

Now that you've completed the training session, we hope that you will share your comments as to how the training materials and activities can be improved. To answer this questionnaire, just choose your "reply" command and the "include original message" option and write your answers below each question. Names will be stripped from your messages before we read your responses, so feel free to be totally honest.

Thank you in advance for all your help!

1. Please rate the following aspects of the training materials and activities based on the scale below:

Scale:
(4) Very helpful
(3) Helpful
(2) Somewhat helpful
(1) Not at all helpful

• Service policies	4___ 3___ 2___ 1___
• Tips for responding to user questions	4___ 3___ 2___ 1___
• Links to Internet sites on Web searching	4___ 3___ 2___ 1___
• Checklist of response components	4___ 3___ 2___ 1___
• Exemplary response	4___ 3___ 2___ 1___
• Practice questions and feedback	4___ 3___ 2___ 1___

2. Please comment on any aspect of the training materials or activities listed above.

3. Overall, was the information presented in the Online Training Course clear and understandable? Please explain.

4. How prepared are you to respond to user inquiries by following the steps presented in the training materials and feedback to your practice questions?

5. What additional information do you think should be included in the training materials?

Following the pilot test and data collection, it is important to revise any aspects of the training program based on results. Although the pilot test is dedicated to identifying problems in the training program, each training session should serve as an opportunity to identify new problems or areas to be revised. See Module 3.4 for more information on ongoing training evaluation techniques.

Once the pilot training program has been revised, you are ready to roll! The next section discusses methods for implementation as well as ongoing management of an AskA training program.

Module 3.3 Summary

This section covers the steps involved in putting the training plan into action.

- The production phase consists of three main steps: create training materials, prepare delivery tools, and pilot test the program.

- When creating training materials, it is important to consider the following issues:

    1. Inform trainees of what they should accomplish by the end of the training program in terms of training objectives.
    2. Create a positive attitude by using attention-getting and confidence-building language and attractive visuals; providing opportunities for interaction; acknowledging participants' busy schedules and expertise; and describing rewards that can be gained from participation.
    3. Provide clear information and examples within the text in order to stress important concepts and to familiarize participants with the ultimate work context.
    4. Provide opportunities for participants to practice job tasks, and offer constructive feedback on participant performance.
    5. Provide resources and support to guide participants in required tasks after the training program.

- When preparing delivery tools, it is important to consider the following issues:

    1. Technical issues of AskA service and participants (e.g., secure Web space, make sure technology is compatible with participants' systems)
    2. Expertise necessary for individuals developing, implementing, and managing tools (e.g., knowledge of HTML, listserv management)
    3. Aesthetic possibilities and limitations of the tool(s) (e.g., information transmitted via e-mail should include a large amount of white space and UNIX-compatible symbols)

- When preparing for and implementing a pilot test, it is important to consider the following issues:

    1. Questions addressing effectiveness of materials, efficiency of the overall session, and extent to which trainees are prepared to perform staff duties.
    2. Methods for eliciting responses to the training program, such as questionnaires or electronic discussion.
    3. Items to be revised before producing the final draft of materials or making final decisions about training activities.

3.4 Implementing and Managing the Training Program

At this point, you should be ready to begin the training program. Training materials have been developed and revised, and delivery tools have been prepared for use. This section discusses important issues to consider in implementation and ongoing management of the training program. Issues include scheduling training events, providing feedback to trainees and staff, and evaluating and revising the training program.

Schedule Training Events

This is the step of the process that most directly affects the participants: training materials are distributed, electronic discussions are held, practice activities are conducted, etc. Although most of the preparation is handled during the production stage, it may be necessary at this point to organize the actual schedule of events. Below is a typical AskA training program schedule with examples from different AskA services (see "Sample AskA Training Models" for more detailed descriptions):

Recruiting and Registration

Most training sessions occur just after an individual or group of new participants becomes part of the service staff or expresses interest in participating. Methods for joining the service as an information specialist or staff member include

- Filling out a Web signup form
- E-mailing the service administrator
- Joining the service as a staff member (through interviewing process, etc.)
- Registering for a university course.

A screening process may also be involved in order to maintain quality of the service and to meet service guidelines. More information on recruiting new participants for an AskA service is found in Module 5: Contributing.

Besides recruiting and signing up new staff members, you may need to make special arrangements for the training program such as setting up e-mail lists for groups of participants and confirming training start dates.

Information Presentation and Orientation

Services may initiate their training sessions by presenting the schedule of activities followed by distribution of a written manual (either online or in print) that explains service policies and outlines job tasks (see Table 3-2 for content frequently covered in AskA training materials). Those services that rely on a written manual as the primary training tool simply point new staff members to the material to begin the training process.

Some services also present information through discussion—either electronic or face-to-face, group or individual. At this point, trainers (staff members delivering the training) can offer advice, and participants can ask questions about specific aspects of their future job tasks.

Practice and Feedback

Practice and feedback activities normally take place after participants are familiar with the information presented in materials and discussion. As previously discussed, this aspect of training is implemented differently by different services to the point where some services do not include practice and feedback as a part of formal training but closely monitor staff work on the job. For instance, some AskA services monitor all outgoing responses from information specialists before they reach the user, while others periodically spot-check responses from information specialists who have successfully completed practice responses during a previous training session.

The elimination of practice and feedback during training quickens the process and allows information specialists to start answering questions immediately; however, it adds time to daily management tasks and decreases the chances for individual improvement unless detailed feedback is offered for each response. (See discussion on providing feedback to trainees and staff later in this module.)

Graduation and Transition

For some services there is a defined transition between the training program and actual service participation (i.e., trainees successfully complete training activities and then take on their roles as service volunteers, experts, moderators, etc.); for other services, the lines between training and service participation are less defined.

Below are some examples of transitions involved in training programs for AskA service information specialists:

- Training participants complete a series of practice exercises: they receive fictional user questions and are expected to respond to them as they would actual user questions. After successfully completing the practice responses, they begin responding directly to incoming user questions. Responses are monitored periodically after being sent to the user. If an information specialist provides quality responses over a period of time, he or she may be asked to monitor others' responses after they are sent to the user. (See "Sample AskA Training Model 3".)

- Training participants respond to incoming user questions in the role of actual "experts." During training, responses are monitored by "trainers" (e.g., current service staff members) before being forwarded to the user. This process continues until the trainers determine that the trainee is ready to bypass the monitoring stage and respond to users directly. (See "Sample AskA Training Models 1 and 4.")

- New information specialists immediately begin responding to incoming user questions in the role of actual "experts" without a formal training program. *All outgoing responses are monitored by service moderators.* "Experts" who provide quality responses over a period of time may be asked to monitor other experts' outgoing responses or may be given other responsibilities or perks. (See "Sample AskA Training Model 2.")

As illustrated above, there are a variety of options available for "graduating" trainees or new staff members into their ultimate service roles. There is no one perfect way to implement this aspect of an AskA training session, but the right balance of events and activities can increase efficiency of service operations. A particular AskA service should choose the order and nature of transitional events according to the following factors:

- **Need for new AskA staff**. Is it desirable to move people through the training process quickly so they can carry out their roles as soon as possible? If so, the training process might allow information specialist trainees to "practice" responding to real incoming user questions. These responses *must* be monitored by knowledgeable staff before being forwarded to the user, which could end up taking more time in the long run.

- **Availability of current staff to implement training**. Are there enough people available to oversee training activities and provide feedback to trainees (one experienced staff member to oversee two or three trainees or new staff members)? Is there an individual or team of staff members dedicated to training? If there is enough time and attention devoted to training, it would be possible to conduct the training process more quickly.

- **Importance of quick response turnaround**. If service policy promises quick turnaround on responses, there may not be enough time for trainees or new staff to "experiment" with real user questions. The time taken for staff to monitor responses before they go to the user may exceed the required time limit. In this case, it is better for novice information specialists to practice on fictional questions until they have achieved training goals and objectives.

- **Difficulty and extent of skills to be learned during training**. If information specialists and staff are expected to carry out an extensive set of tasks or must learn a set of new skills or knowledge (e.g., use of technology, subject knowledge, research skills), it will be advantageous to devote a significant amount of time for formal training. This will result in fewer mistakes and less monitoring in the long run.

Providing Feedback to Trainees and Staff

Providing feedback is one of the most important aspects of a training program. It offers each participant personal attention and constructive support for improvement. Some feedback may be oral (for instance, in a face-to-face context) or written; written feedback may include open-ended comments or symbols from a grading scheme (e.g., 5 = more than expected, 1 = extensive revision necessary, etc.). (See "Sample AskA Training Models" for examples of specific feedback methods.) Regardless of the method and timing of delivery, feedback should both guide and motivate participants and staff to perform tasks successfully (as defined in training objectives). In order for feedback to be helpful, it should include the following components:

Positive Statement

Start the conversation by praising the trainee or staff member for some positive aspect of his or her work. For instance, highlight the information specialist's friendly tone and then point out the fact that he didn't include the user's original message in the response.

> This was a good try for your first response. The Web site you suggested does a great job of explaining the history of the typewriter keyboard. The illustrations are also very helpful.
>
> You expressed genuine interest in the student's question. This can help to motivate students. It was also a good idea to suggest Infotrac and a local physician in addition to Internet resources.

Objectives

Remind trainees or staff of the objectives they should achieve, including components to include in user responses and other specific service procedures, noting which ones were achieved and which ones were not.

> You included almost all of the components of the response checklist: you included the original message, greeted the student by name, included a factual response, and cited your resources. One thing you left out was the archive account address in the carbon copy field.

It also helps to explain the importance of including certain components to link training objectives to real AskA service situations.

> It is important to include the search engine and search terms you used to find the Web sites so users can learn to conduct Internet searches on their own.

Tips and Suggestions for Improvement

Sometimes trainees or staff members have difficulty performing certain tasks because they are still new to the required technology or other aspects of the job. Although related information may be covered in the training materials, it is still helpful to reinforce or expand on specific concepts in response to mistakes or questions of individual participants.

> **Include original message**. This can usually be done by selecting options for "reply" and then "include original message." Check your e-mail program for directions.

> Instead of typing Web addresses in your responses, another alternative is to copy the URL from the Web site and paste it directly into the message—if you have the capability to keep your e-mail and Web browser open at the same time. This will help to avoid incorrect Web addresses due to typographical errors.

In addition to providing tips for performing certain technical tasks, it is helpful to provide general suggestions for improving one's work, such as responses to users. These suggestions may address the aesthetic or educational value of service products.

> One suggestion for making responses easier to read is to physically separate ideas from each other. For instance, start a new line when talking about a new resource, like this:
>
> • Bill Nye Episode Guide: DESERTS
>   *http://nyelabs.kcts.org/nyeverse/episode/e72.html*
> • Deserts
>   *http://www.cuug.ab.ca:8001/~animal/deserts.html*

> For this particular question, I would suggest referring the student to the archive. Some of our math experts have already written excellent responses on the order of operations that could serve as supplemental resources for the student.

Availability of Support

No matter how well the trainee or new staff member is performing, it is important to let each participant know that an administrator or other staff member is available for help on an ongoing basis. This communicates to staff that the service is always looking to improve and that individual attention and support are available when needed. This can be done by including a quick statement at the end of a feedback message (e.g., "Let me know if you have any questions.")

Ongoing Evaluation and Revision of Training Program

As a service matures, training materials and programs should be altered according to feedback from information specialists and support staff (e.g., common questions or confusion about particular processes), observation of staff performance (e.g., quality of information specialists' responses), and other factors relating to user satisfaction. Developing a training program is an evolving process that responds to needs as they are identified. Evaluation and revision of the training program will complement the overall evaluation efforts of the AskA service (see Module 6).

The ongoing evaluation of the training program is an extension of the pilot testing process (see Module 3.3). The difference is that an ongoing evaluation process can address the impact of training materials and activities on staff performance over a period of time. This provides an opportunity to monitor work such as responses to user questions and identify common issues among different staff members and situations. The following issues (as well as others) may signal the need for evaluation and revision of training materials and activities:

- Staff performance (e.g., lack of a particular component in information specialists' responses, inability of moderator staff to provide effective feedback to information specialists)
- Development of new tasks (changes in procedures) due to new software, improved processes, etc.
- Feedback from staff (e.g., after some experience, staff members may discover they would be more comfortable or more successful performing tasks if certain skills were developed)

Evaluation Methods and Tools

Evaluation methods for AskA training programs can range from formal plans (e.g., a focused assessment of training materials, activities, etc.) to informal activities (e.g., day-to-day observation of staff, unsolicited feedback from users). Figure 3-5 is an example of a Web-based questionnaire used to elicit feedback from information specialists following their participation in a training session.

Figure 3-5 Training Questionnaire on the Web (sample excerpt)

Information Specialist Training Questionnaire

It is time to revise our training program. Now that you've worked as an information specialist for a few months, we hope that you will share your comments as to how training materials and activities can be improved. To answer this questionnaire, just complete the questions below and click the "submit" button at the bottom of the page.

Thank you in advance for all your help!

1. How well did the training materials and activities prepare you to do the following (please rate on a scale from 1 to 4 where 1 = very well and 4 = not at all):
respond to user questions: ___
use service information resources: ___
use service work-flow software program: ___

2. What additional tasks or issues do you feel you were unprepared for upon beginning work with the service?
3. What information would be most useful to you now in completing your required tasks?

SUBMIT

Once information is collected from the training program evaluation, the data should be analyzed. Services can revise programs as necessary. Depending on evaluation results, services may revise training manuals to include further explanation of certain procedures, add more opportunity for practice during the training program, or adjust other training components to better accommodate staff in effectively preparing for tasks involved in AskA service participation. See Module 6: Evaluation, for more suggestions on conducting evaluation of the overall AskA service.

Module 3.4 Summary

This section covers the steps involved in implementing and managing the training program on an ongoing basis.

- Ongoing implementation and management of an AskA training program involves scheduling training events, providing feedback to trainees and staff, and evaluating and revising the training program.

- Many services include the following training events in the implementation of their training programs:

    1. Recruiting new staff and "registering" them for participation in the service or training program
    2. Presenting information (training content) and orientation to the service (e.g., policies and procedures, etc.)
    3. Practice activities and feedback on performance
    4. "Graduation," or a transition from training or trial status to official staff member or volunteer of the service.

- Effective feedback from experienced staff members guides and motivates trainees and new staff to improve their performance. The following components should be included in feedback communications:

    1. Statements praising positive aspects of the work
    2. Reminder of objectives outlined in training and statement of progress in terms of achieving the objectives
    3. Tips and suggestions for improvement
    4. Statements offering individual support during and after training.

- An ongoing evaluation and revision process allows the AskA service to determine the impact of the training program on staff performance and ways to improve components. Ongoing evaluation and revision involves the following:

    1. Identifying opportunities for evaluation and revision
    2. Gathering evaluative information through observation, instrument distribution, etc.
    3. Revising training program based on evaluation results.

Sample AskA Training Models

The following pages include descriptions of training programs of existing AskA services. These training programs serve as models for AskA service training, representing some of the possible methods for distributing training materials, conducting training activities and other events involved in preparing information specialists to answer user questions. (Methods for training support staff are mentioned when available.)

AskA Training Model 1
Ask Dr. Math, The Math Forum, Swarthmore College
http://forum.swarthmore.edu/dr.math/

Training for Volunteer Experts ("Math Doctors")

Recruiting and Registration

The Ask Dr. Math Web site contains a section that introduces the service and links to a signup form to become part of the volunteer math doctor team. Potential participants can access this information through links from the main service Web site. For each new volunteer who signs up to become a math doctor, an account is created in the service system.

Information Presentation and Orientation

Each new volunteer receives a message from service administrators that explains basic information about the service and asks the volunteer to review the online manual, "Guide to Writing Responses" (Foster, 1998). This guide covers technical issues (e.g., format for including math symbols and graphics in responses, methods for selecting questions from the queue for response, required components for responses); quality issues (e.g., writing clearly and with a friendly tone, explaining reasons for performing certain math formulas, fostering user creativity); and information on available resources (e.g., FAQ, archive, other sites). New participants are encouraged to become familiar with service resources that can aid in response writing, including the archive and FAQs.

Practice and Feedback

New "math doctors" begin answering incoming user questions but send their responses to an account called the "Holding Tank." Responses in the "Holding Tank" are reviewed by experienced staff members or service administrators. Responses that meet service requirements are forwarded to the user; those which do not meet all requirements are returned to the "math doctor" for revision. If the math doctor is unable to revise the message, an administrator will rewrite it and add his or her name to the response.

Trainers look for responses that contain clear writing styles and good answering techniques and reflect understanding of math concepts. They provide feedback to new math doctors by offering examples and explanations and encouraging conversation. Trainers keep notepads on each new volunteer to track their progress during the training process.

Transitions and Rewards

Volunteer notepads are reviewed periodically to determine which volunteers should receive "tenure" (the opportunity to send responses directly to the user). New volunteers who have consistently produced inadequate responses may be asked not to continue with the service.

Training for Administrators and Other Trainers

Currently there is no formal program for training staff other than new volunteers. However, discussions are held about the training process, and the service may provide a train-the-trainer program as it expands its training staff.

See Module 2 for complete Ask Dr. Math case study.

AskA Training Model 2
MAD Scientist Network, Washington University Medical School
http://www.madsci.org

Training for Volunteer Experts (Scientists)

Recruiting and Registration

Individuals interested in serving as science experts complete a signup form on the service's Web site. Information captured on the form includes contact information, professional or academic position, and areas of interest and expertise within science and math. Each form is reviewed by a service administrator who sends each candidate an introductory message containing information on the service's Web site contents and question-answer procedures.

Information Presentation and Orientation

The official "training" process involves an online manual containing procedures for answering questions, administrative information (scheduling, etc.), and using World Wide Web resources in responses (links, searching for sites, etc.; MAD Scientist Network, 1997b). Trainees are also introduced to the online interfaces for submitting answers; this information contains additional material to support the response process following training in the form of a job aid. Important points stressed during training include expected response components and turnaround time (e.g., respond within seven days after receiving a question or notify administrator of inability to field the question).

Ongoing Practice and Feedback

Although the training process does not involve practice activities, all responses undergo a screening process before they are sent to the user. All responses from all experts are reviewed by "moderators" for quality and appropriateness and then graded on a scale from 1 to 5 (where 1 = "great answer" and 5 = "requires heavy editing to be useful"). Grades are used for tracking an expert's performance overall and within specific categories and for indicating quality of responses in the archive for weeding purposes. Grades are not shared with the individual experts.

Moderators provide feedback to experts when they notify them that their answers have been placed on the Web server. If the response is placed "on hold," moderators inform experts of the corrections or additional information needed for the response to meet appropriate standards.

Transitions and Rewards

Experts who demonstrate quality responses over a period of time may be asked to serve as moderators. They may also be highlighted on the service Web site on a page called the "MadSci Hall of Fame" (*http://www.madsci.wustl.edu/madhof.html*), which includes exemplary experts' biographies, research interests, and other information. In the future, the service may be able to offer Web space to some experts so that they can develop their materials.

Training for "Moderators"

Moderators of the service review all incoming questions to the service as well as all outgoing responses from the experts. Each moderator is responsible for the questions and responses in one or more subject areas.

Moderator training consists of an online manual (MAD Scientist Network, 1997a) highlighting required background and expectations of moderators, time commitments, information on using the moderating interface, and tips for reviewing questions, reviewing and "grading" responses, and reviewing and recycling unanswered questions. Moderators are also referred to internal service Web resources for becoming familiar with service.

See Module 2 for complete MAD Scientist Network case study.

AskA Training Model 3
KidsConnect, American Association of School Librarians
http://www.ala.org/ICONN/AskKC.html

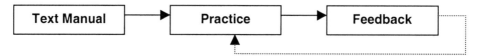

Training for School Library Media Specialist Volunteers

KidsConnect volunteers are library media specialists who answer general subject questions from K–12 students. All new volunteers undergo a formal training process before they are able to answer incoming student questions.

Recruiting and Registration

Volunteers are recruited through postings to professional school library listservs, presentations at school library conferences, and professional publications. Dates of upcoming training sessions are included in some of these communications. Interested individuals contact the service coordinator indicating possible dates for participation in a training session.

The coordinator organizes interested individuals into training groups of 5–10 people and confirms training start dates with each individual. At the start of a training session, the coordinator distributes an introductory e-mail message to each member of the session (via a distribution list) outlining the schedule for the session (e.g., read materials, receive first practice question, respond to practice question, etc.) and location of online training materials (along with login and password for accessing documents). Training participants are encouraged to send an e-mail message to the list introducing themselves in terms of their current professional positions (including grade levels served) and interests in order to build a sense of community among members.

Information Presentation and Orientation

The first activity of each training session involves reading the online manual and supplementary materials. The online manual contains information on the service, volunteer responsibilities, course objectives, required skills and technical capabilities, descriptions and examples of guidelines for responding to student inquiries, and directions for practice activities. Supplementary information provides tips on using the Internet as a research tool and responding to student inquiries. The supplementary document is intended as a guide during and after the training session.

Practice and Feedback

On the day scheduled, the service coordinator distributes the first practice question to each participant. (If participants complete the online manual and supplement earlier than this scheduled date, they can request the first practice question via a Web-based form.) Participants respond to the first practice question (a previously asked student question) using the procedures outlined in the training materials. Participants send their responses to the service coordinator or other trainer who in turn provides them with detailed feedback. After their first practice response has been assessed, participants receive their second practice question from the coordinator or trainer (this is done on an individual basis). The practice-feedback cycle continues until participants' responses are acceptable and participants feel comfortable composing responses. Training participants normally receive about three or four practice questions before being asked to join a team of active volunteers.

Once a volunteer is part of an active question answering team, he or she receives periodic feedback from his or her team leader, an individual who mentors and manages a group of volunteers. Periodic feedback is less involved than feedback received during training; the purpose is to verify that required response components are included and that questions are answered appropriately.

Transition and Rewards

After trainees have successfully responded to three or four practice questions, they are invited to join an existing team of volunteers who answer questions from students of the same grade level on the same volunteer schedule.

Volunteers who provide quality responses over a period of time are sometimes asked to serve as team leaders, volunteers who oversee responses from members of a given team.

Team Leader Training

Team leaders are volunteers who have already undergone the main training program and have successfully answered student questions for some time. Training them for their duties as team leaders consists of pointing them to a short online manual detailing their responsibilities and a guide for providing feedback to volunteers.

See Module 4 for complete KidsConnect case study.

AskA Training Model 4
AskERIC, Educational Resources Information Center
http://www.askeric.org

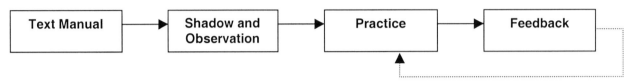

Training for Network Information Specialists

AskERIC Network Information Specialists (NIS) provide responses to questions regarding educational theory and practice. NIS are located in several different clearinghouses of the Educational Resources Information Center (ERIC) system. This training model represents training activities in the central AskERIC office at the ERIC Clearinghouse on Information & Technology based at Syracuse University.

Recruiting and Registration

NIS are hired through the ERIC system as paid staff of an individual ERIC clearinghouse. Upon start of the position, each NIS is taken through an individual training process depending on individual clearinghouse practice.

Information Presentation and Orientation

Initial training consists of reading print and online manuals outlining service history, mission, and supporting organizations; question-answer policies and procedures; technology basics (e-mail, system software and hardware); database searching (service-specific resources); and Internet searching (System-wide guide to AskERIC question answering, 1998). (Materials addressing general system issues are shared across clearinghouses.) In addition to reading training materials, NIS are given a general orientation to the specific work environment.

Shadowing

After the new NIS has a chance to read through the training materials, he or she shadows a few veteran NIS and observes the question-answer process firsthand. During the shadowing period, new NIS learn tips and techniques for question answering, including issues of tone and appearance of e-mail responses.

Practice and Feedback

After the shadowing period, new NIS respond to questions on their own. For about two weeks, responses are reviewed by veteran NIS before going out to the user. Ongoing feedback is offered to NIS on a periodic basis.

See Module 5 for complete AskERIC case study.

AskA Training Model 5
Internet Public Library, University of Michigan School of Information
http://www.ipl.org

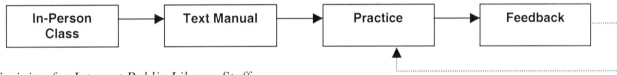

Training for Internet Public Library Staff

The Internet Public Library (IPL) is a project of the University of Michigan School of Information that provides Internet users with access to resources as well as digital reference service. The IPL serves all audiences with special attention to youth needs. Online training resources such as policy manuals are available to staff who maintain the project and professional librarians who answer digital reference questions. IPL's main training efforts have been spent on educating those external to the project about digital librarianship and IPL policies in order to recruit new staff and information specialists and to produce new IPL resources. This training effort is delivered in the form of a graduate course through the University of Michigan School of Information.

Registration

Students register for the digital librarianship course through the university. Many students who take the class continue with the Internet Public Library (IPL) service as a reference volunteer or staff member.

Information Presentation

The course is dedicated to developing resources and providing question-answer support for the IPL as well as discussing the nature of librarianship in a networked environment. Face-to-face class meetings provide a forum to discuss IPL service procedures and technology; skills and issues involved in digital librarianship; Internet searching; and logistical issues regarding student projects. The class has been taught via distance with initial face-to-face interaction and then continued through listserv discussion and individual project work (see Practice and Feedback below).

Supporting materials include information on question answering policy (preparing a response, mandatory response components, etc.); reference response style guidelines (e.g., providing instruction to the user, writing with a friendly tone); using the IPL question-answer interface; and tips for finding and evaluating Internet resources.

<u>Practice and Feedback</u>

The emphasis of the course is on practical experience that often occurs outside of the classroom: collection development projects, question answering, visiting the IPL lab. The main practice component of the course is the students' question-answering experience. During the course, each student is responsible for answering 8–10 questions per week according to IPL question answering policy. Experienced IPL volunteers or staff team up with groups of students to provide support and feedback on the question-answering process as well as on individual student responses. This monitoring stage ends once students become regular volunteers (if they choose to do so).

Electronic Reference: Service Issues and Necessary Skills

by Sara Weissman

The Morris County (NJ) Library began as an experiment in electronic reference in January 1997. Intended as a six-month project, the service was so manageable that it has continued. In 14 months, volume has risen from one or two questions a week to two or three a day. Questions are posted to two staff members with one reference librarian as the lead responder or referrer. The head of the reference department serves as backup in absence of a primary staff member and monitors the volume and nature of the questions to determine impact on overall work-flow.

Staff training has not been a part of Morris County Library's electronic reference service. This is due to the fact that the librarian handling electronic reference has had a significant amount of experience in academic and public reference (14 years), electronic communications (moderated chat rooms and bulletin boards as AOL online volunteer for three years), and Internet training for teachers, librarians, and the public since 1993. During her experiences, she has become of aware of specific issues related to electronic reference and the skills necessary for dealing with these issues. The table below offers issues and skills based on the electronic reference done through April 1998. [22]

Table 3-6 Electronic Reference Service Issues and Required Skills for Morris County Library, N J.

Event or Problem	Service Issues	Skills Required
1. Service reaches worldwide user base including users from India, Brazil, and Philippines.	Define patron universe: • Who will or won't you serve? • To what extent will international users be served (e.g., short answer, referral, transmit materials, etc.)?	Staff must know how to • Read domain names (country end codes) of e-mail addresses and use WHOIS or convert domain to Web URL to identify source area of query. • Use tools like *American Library Directory, Special Collections*, and *LibWeb* to locate remote patrons' nearest collections.
2. Service receives vague, ill-worded query.	Identify steps to take in initial response to patron: • Individual follow-up or template? • Re-statement of query only or initial information provided?	Staff must be able to recognize that • Patrons often have no concept of the possibilities of information, so query is tentative. • Query may be from patron writing in a second language.

[22] This table outlines skills required in daily activities of one electronic reference service. These skills can be translated into instructional objectives for training information specialists of this service and others.

Event or Problem	Service Issues	Skills Required
3. Incoming question refers to a subject not best served by library resources (e.g., social services, law, quality of life issues, etc.).	Define service scope: • Serve as gateway to other agency information? • Does an electronic presence carry with it an imperative to help?	Staff should recognize when to • Refer queries or mediate acquisition of information. • Decline question politely and helpfully.
4. Patron seems to expect entire answer to be Internet-based.	Identify range of source material from which answers will be drawn and to which patrons will be referred.	Staff should know how to • Explicate universes of information. • Explain limits of different types of information resources.
5. Patron seems to expect immediate service.	Explain probable turnaround time to patron.	Staff should be able to • Understand patrons' misapprehension of electronic reference as 24-hour service. • Provide possible information or refer to immediate sources, if any.
6. Requested information cannot be readily provided electronically.	Define procedures for amount and format of transmittal of information.	Staff should be able to • Provide available information • Explain possible additional resources or information • Offer suggestions and routines for non-electronic materials acquisition (interlibrary loan, local collections or agencies)
7. Service receives repeat query from same patron.	Devise tracking system for queries answered and respondent.	Staff should be able to • Recognize that e-patrons send queries to several libraries or lose answers through mail errors. • Compose neutral response asking if material is required again.
8. Service receives repeat question from several patrons.	Identify processes for providing information on common topics: • Keep an FAQ file. • Write and point to a Web page. • Prepare and provide an information packet.	Staff should be able to • Recognize repeat queries. • Consult with colleagues on developing responses to common queries.

132

Event or Problem	Service Issues	Skills Required
9. Lack of closure to service-patron exchange.	Identify procedure for following up with exchanges: • How often? • By individual or template mailing?	Staff should recognize characteristics of • Completion of exchange. • Patron satisfaction.
10. Nature of queries causes staff to grow impatient.	Provide techniques to motivate staff and prevent burnout: • Rotate e-ref staff. • Balance electronic reference with time spent with local patrons.	Staff should • Recognize signs of irritability and burnout. • Decline e-ref responsibility rather than provide hasty, impatient responses to patrons.
11. Satisfied patron threatens to abuse the service.	Create policy regarding limits of service and explaining reasons for such policy.	Staff should recognize when to: • Politely decline queries. • Reroute queries to more appropriate agencies or offices.
12. Staff feels unable to answer question.	• Track and analyze unanswered queries to gauge service and collection. • Develop response method or form that respects patrons' questions but explains why institution or service cannot provide answer. • Suggest information and individual or agency that may help answer question.	Staff should be able to recognize when questions indicate • User's misunderstanding of the service. • Deficiency in the collection or in staff training.

Sara Weissman, _weissman@main.morris.org_, is reference librarian at Morris County Library in Whippany, NJ (_http://www.gti.net/mocolib1/MCL.html_).

Module 4

Informing
Planning
Training
Prototyping
Contributing
Evaluating

Prototyping

Creating and Testing AskA Services in a Controlled Environment

Module Profile

Once an AskA plan is created, the service should be tested in a controlled environment. Organizations that have launched services to the public too soon have experienced question overload, sometimes to the point of having to discontinue service. Prototypes allow organizations to expand gradually with the opportunity to adjust plans (including policy and procedures) based on initial feedback and experience. This module is designed to assist organizations in testing and developing an AskA service according to an AskA plan. At the conclusion of this module, you will be able to achieve the following goal:

Goal   Create a prototype and conduct a pilot test of an AskA service.

Prerequisites Before prototyping an AskA service, an organization should be able to
1. Collect information on the general digital reference field and existing AskA services (see Module 1: Informing).
2. Determine the best way to build and maintain digital reference service within the organization (see Module 2: Planning).
3. Plan, produce, implement, and manage training programs for service staff and information specialists (see Module 3: Training). Note: Services may implement the training program pilot test during the prototyping stage.

Objectives   At the completion of this module, you will be able to achieve the following objectives:
1. Understand the purpose of creating a prototype of an AskA service.
2. Identify common factors in prototypes of AskA services.
3. Describe important components for pilot testing an AskA service prototype.
4. Identify issues and questions to be addressed during a pilot test.
5. Revise prototype based on pilot test results.

4.1 Prototyping the AskA Service

The step between planning and implementing an AskA service is a crucial one. The prototyping stage represents a period of incubation when the service functions with some of its planned components but in an atmosphere of formative testing—with the possibility of revision and expansion. Some organizations and individuals have learned the hard lesson of publicizing an AskA service before important features are tested and before an underlying structure is in place to support it. This has resulted in such an uncontrollable number of questions that a service is forced to eliminate its opportunity for gradual growth—and, in some cases, must discontinue altogether. Prototyping can help an organization plan for service growth to avoid such disasters.

Given that many AskA services begin as experimental efforts, the prototype phase is not always considered separate from the overall development process. Many services seem to begin small and grow naturally based on increased demand and resources. Those services that begin with a prototype are able to try strategies in controlled environments (through trial and error) before offering service to the larger population. This section discusses the concept of prototyping as it relates to the development of AskA services and offers suggestions and examples for creating an AskA prototype prior to conducting a pilot test. Although the Training phase is placed before Prototyping in this text, the development of a training program may take place after the prototyping stage when issues of policy and procedure are more firmly established or may occur in conjunction with the prototyping stage (e.g., the training program pilot test may be implemented with the service prototype pilot test).

Prototyping: General Definitions and Concepts

The practice of prototyping—the development of an incomplete but usable version of a product—has been used in a variety of contexts including engineering, software development, and manufacturing. Prototypes can assist developers in assessing a product by providing feedback without requiring the expense of a full development cycle (Jones & Merrill, 1992). One approach to prototyping involves a process of quickly building and testing a prototype early on in the development process in order to make more focused decisions regarding development of the final product. This is referred to as **rapid prototyping**, a practice that has become increasingly widespread in software development as a way to ensure that user needs are adequately met before the final product is in their hands (Mullin, 1990). Rapid prototyping is considered more flexible than traditional techniques and can be more cost efficient.

The concept of rapid prototyping works well in the context of building AskA services, because the nature of AskA service is one of constant change. As previously mentioned, most services tend to start out on a smaller scale naturally; this is due to a variety of factors: low supply of resources and funding; question of future commitment on the part of the managing organization; slow start to publicity; etc. As the service grows, user questions and other *detectors* (see Module 2: Planning) will constantly inform the processes and the ultimate service. In this way, an AskA service is in a constant iterative state as opposed to a product that is developed and ultimately sold in its final form.

Prototyping AskA Services

Although prototypes of AskA services are more abstract than those of software or other types of products, they can still serve to provide organizations with important information before a service "goes live." AskA prototypes involve manipulation of detectors, rules, and effectors to create a manageable set of factors. In other words, an AskA prototype is created by adapting the original AskA plan to temporarily run on a smaller scale. For instance, an AskA plan may indicate that a service will use 500 engineering experts from all over the country ("Resources: Human Resources") to answer questions of K–12 students all over the world ("Effectors"[23]). The AskA prototype could include 10 graduate engineering students from Carnegie Mellon University with a user base of students from local Pittsburgh high schools.

When creating or establishing a prototype of an AskA service, it is primarily important to consider the manipulation of the AskA plan that is least expensive and time and labor intensive. However, the prototype must still represent the planned service adequately enough to provide useful information.

Common Factors in AskA Prototypes

Some AskA services have deliberately created prototypes, while others began naturally on a smaller scale and developed over time. New AskA services can learn lessons from both experiences in terms of original service structure and eventual growth. Services can use a combination of the following factors (and others) to create their AskA prototype.

---

[23] While a service may have the means to gather information on students (Detectors: Users), the actual service (in terms of responses to users) is considered an output (Effectors).

Controlled Group of Experts (Information Specialists)

One common method for creating a prototype is by controlling the number of experts who will answer user questions. By keeping this initial group small, service administrators can control time spent on training, question distribution, assessment of responses, and other management issues, while taking the opportunity to test the overall process. Academic environments are especially conducive to prototyping AskA services in that they can supply organizations with available sets of students, faculty, and staff eager to share their expertise with inquiring users. The following are examples of methods taken by existing AskA services to control their original expert groups:

- **Representatives from sponsoring higher education institution (students, faculty, staff, etc.).** Ask Dr. Math originally launched its service in 1994 with a small expert base of students from Swarthmore College, the institution housing the service and its parent project, the Math Forum. Today, Ask Dr. Math has over 225 volunteer "math doctors" from all over the world. (See case study, "The Evolution of Ask Dr. Math.") The MAD Scientist Network, of Washington University Medical School, began in September 1995 with an expert base of 25 scientists (professors and graduate and medical students) from the medical school; this number quickly grew to 40 scientists by the next month. MAD Scientist administrators posted fliers at the medical school in order to recruit the scientists. MAD Scientist's expert base has expanded to over 600 scientists from around the world. (See case study, "Planning an Ask-A-Scientist Service.")

- **Ultimate expert pool, limited number of participants.** KidsConnect, from the American Association of School Librarians, gradually grew its volunteer base through a deliberate pilot effort. Prior to the service's "go live" date, interested experts (library media specialists) responded to requests for volunteers posted on a professional listserv, and the KidsConnect Coordinator organized a series of four pilot and training sessions. By the time the service went public, KidsConnect had 30 volunteers (starting with an original group of 10); today the service has over 200 volunteers. (See case study, "Pilot Testing the KidsConnect Service.")

- **Existing service staff.** AskERIC, of the Educational Resources Information Center, began in 1992 with two full-time staff members who responded to user questions and performed general service management tasks. Gradually the staff base expanded to over 50 educational information specialists. (See case study, "Managing Growing Numbers of Questions for AskERIC.")

In addition to gradually increasing a service's expert base, services should incrementally increase support staff (e.g., moderators, team leaders, etc.) over time. AskA prototypes can include small numbers of support staff with plans to expand.

Controlled Group of Users

Some services begin with a limited user base in order to control the number of questions coming into the system. Methods of limiting users can involve targeting communities that are accessible to the organization. Like the controlled group of experts, this works especially well for academic communities where inquisitive students are in abundance. Services have also found it possible to limit users to those in a particular geographic location. Some examples include the following:

- **Users from experts' communities**. Library media specialist volunteers from the KidsConnect prototype responded to questions of students in their own schools in order to practice the required tasks and simulate the question-answer process.

- **Users from service and organization community**. The MAD Scientist Network originally created its Web site to allow K–12 students from St. Louis public schools to ask science questions of faculty, staff, and students at Washington University (part of the "Young Scientist Program" *medinfo.wustl.edu/~ysp/*, a student-run program at the medical school that aims to increase the science literacy of area K–12 students through hands-on learning).

- **Users from limited geographic area**. AskERIC selected three state networks to post and highlight its service. It chose NYSERNet in New York, SENDIT in North Dakota, and TENET in Texas. These state networks were the most developed and provided the greatest support to K–12 educators (AskERIC's population) at the time.

Minimal Advertising

In the prototype stage, organizations should be extremely careful about publicizing their services. It is advised that services do not offer methods for capturing user questions other than those from pilot groups during the prototyping stage. It is important that advertising efforts be directed only towards those users and participants who have been identified in the prototype.

Some services may choose not to publicize at all until the service is ready to go public. Others may choose to make potential users and participants aware of current efforts as a way of building enthusiasm and support for the service. Publicizing at this point is best kept to professional forums where organizations can increase awareness of and enthusiasm for the upcoming available service; common methods include presenting and exhibiting at professional conferences and announcements on professional discussion groups. See Module 5: Contributing, for examples of publicizing active services.

Available Technology

Obviously it would be most favorable to select and implement a system that could be easily adapted to "live" service from the prototype. Since it is difficult to predict the changes in service structure as well as changes in technology, many services start with one system and then migrate to another. (See Module 5: Contributing, for tips and suggestions on selecting or creating software for AskA services.)

Below are some examples of technology solutions employed by AskA services during their prototyping stages:

- **Borrowed server space.** Services may seek Web space from an external provider in order to get up and running. For instance, the National Museum of American Art (NMAA) Reference Desk originally housed its site on America Online (AOL). This arrangement worked well, because AOL was local to NMAA and the AskA service originally lacked funds for staff and equipment of its own. (See case study, "Getting Underway: The Virtual Reference Desk at the National Museum of American Art.")

- **Limit user interface.** Some existing services began by using e-mail only and eventually migrated to a Web site (on which they provided user query forms as well as information resources). Working in this mode during the prototyping stage helped these services to focus more on the question-answer process and policies and less on resource creation and dissemination.

- **Create original software.** While clearly the most time consuming and talent dependent, this solution has been used by some services in order to automate specific service functions. During the prototyping stage, the software is built, tested, and revised. The MAD Scientist Network created its own PERL-based software package called *Moderator*, which was built in 1995 and has evolved as the service grew (Bry, 1997).

There are some important factors in selecting software in the prototype phase. Software selected should incorporate four aspects as highlighted in Table 4-1:

Table 4-1 Factors in Selecting Software for AskA Service Prototype

Aspect	Facet	Example
Open: Open software allows for growth and change. It conforms to standards that are developed in the "public" space. By conforming to open standards, an organization becomes less dependent on a single software provider that may radically change or discontinue a product. An example of this would be proprietary mail systems that have either been discontinued or changed to adapt to open Internet standards. This does not imply that proprietary solutions are inherently bad (or even more risky), but rather serves as a caution when one is shopping for software. Open software can also refer to an organization's ability to modify the product as needed. In many cases software is provided with source code, allowing an individual or team to rewrite portions of the code.	Supports open standards	TCP/IP for networking standards. Simple Mail Transfer Protocol (SMTP) and Post Office Protocol (POP) for e-mail.
	Can add features or customization	APACHE Web sever or the support of the Common Gateway Interface (CGI) for Web programming.
Scalable: Prototyping provides valuable learning opportunities to AskA services. In many ways, the prototyping period will be the longest time a service has to systematically think about the AskA service. If this learning does not occur with the final software selection, it is an opportunity lost. Therefore, a software package that can be scaled up for implementation is preferable. So choose a system that can accommodate final growth projections; thinking big early will save time, money, and effort later.	Can grow as the service grows	Buy software that can license more users as the service grows; that way you can pay as you grow. For free software look for performance issues and multi-user capabilities.

141

Aspect	Facet	Example
Supportable: The largest question when selecting software is who will take care of the product after purchase. Support is the number one issue when making a buying or adoption decision. An organization can choose to pay for support, making bugs, fixes, and maintenance someone else's problem; it can hire an expert to keep the software running; or it can look for an active support community that is willing to help out.	Paid support	Support contracts and toll-free telephone number support. Some software packages include this support in the price; others offer it for an additional cost.
	Internal support	Finding software development and support expertise can be difficult and expensive. However, having someone on payroll (or a responsible volunteer) can provide the maximum support and customization ability.
	Community or user support	This is how the Internet was founded, and there are still many products (such as the Linux operating system) that utilize a community of experts who are willing to volunteer the knowledge and assistance.
Internet enabled: Digital reference services aren't by definition Internet services. It just turns out that the Internet is the only game in town to link to communities beyond the walls of an organization, such as the K–12 community. The irony is that many help desk solutions you can buy don't fully support the Internet. Software selected must be able to take questions from the Internet (in the form of either e-mail or Web pages) and must be able to post the answers back to the Internet (once again with e-mail or the Web).	Web	Can the software take and return questions via the Web? Will answers be archived automatically in a Web-accessible knowledge base? For many users the Web is a better alternative to ask and get questions than e-mail. Public library users, for example, may not have individual e-mail accounts.
	E-mail	Can the software accept questions via e-mail?

There is still a lot of development to be done in the area of AskA software. Standards and available "off the shelf" solutions are rare (if not nonexistent). Most organizations will need to borrow existing code. The outlook for software is, however, bright. The government and other organizations are hard at work developing software for this very purpose. Also, as companies see the importance of retrieving, tracking, and answering questions using the Internet, more software options will become available.

142

4.2 Conducting the Pilot Test

Once a prototype is built, it needs to be tested. An AskA plan and its stripped-down prototype may look good on paper, but what about implementation? How will procedures be carried out? Are policies realistic?

The pilot test helps to answer these questions by allowing services to implement the prototype in a controlled manner. In other words the service will run using a limited number of experts or users (or both) and incorporating any other factors. In conducting the pilot test, special attention is paid to feedback of participants in terms of making decisions for revision of the AskA plan. This section discusses activities involved in the prototyping stage in order to capture important feedback.

Ingredients for Successful Pilot Test

There are no hard and fast rules for conducting a pilot test of an AskA service. The actual events and components will depend on the service's original plan and prototype. However, the two most important factors to consider in any AskA service pilot test are control of the overall testing effort and an open forum for communication between pilot participants and service administrators.

Controlling the Testing Effort. While some services may loosely consider their beginning stage as a pilot, it is most helpful to plan some parameters by which to conduct a formal pilot test effort. This can work by organizing a specific timeframe for the pilot to occur and setting an agenda. Just like any other type of evaluation, the pilot test should begin by identifying specific objectives to guide the effort. The service should consider what it wants to accomplish by conducting the pilot test. In other words what are the major questions that the service hopes to answer in this test of service? Examples include

- Will the software support the planned question-answer procedure?
- Will the training program adequately prepare information specialists and staff for their roles?
- Are service policies feasible?

More specific questions for pilot testing are listed in the section "Questions Asked During the Pilot Test."

Providing Opportunities for Communication. It is extremely important to allow an open line of communication between all participants and service administrators. While observation of events is helpful, it is participant feedback that can offer insight into the types of issues that could arise after a public launch of the service. For instance, are the expectations of volunteer experts realistic (e.g., time limits, required steps for composing responses)? Are users satisfied with the types of responses offered? Are there any political issues that may cause individuals to decline participation as experts or cause potential users to not take advantage of the service? These and other issues can be raised and discussed with pilot participants before the service is launched. Communication should occur throughout the pilot, but it is also helpful to arrange for a formal "debriefing" in order to summarize and resolve important issues.

Methods for encouraging communication include the following:
- Survey—by e-mail or Web to get initial reaction to ideas, concerns, etc.
- Listserv discussion—some standard questions, but encourage discussion among participants. Gives participants sense of ownership in project—important for volunteers who don't get repaid in other ways.
- Face-to-face meetings or focus groups—if all participants are onsite (or in close proximity).

Questions Asked During the Pilot Test

Although many of these issues will be raised in the planning stage (see Module 2), the pilot test may raise the following questions regarding **question-answer policy and procedure:**

- What resources should experts use when responding to user questions?
- What technical capabilities should be required of experts and users?
- What should be the general nature of a response (e.g., factual answer vs. pointers to resources)?
- What components are necessary to include in a response?
- What is the sequence of events taken in responding to a user query?
- How much time does the question-answer process take?

Other questions may relate to the **comfort level of experts or information specialists** in responding to user queries (these questions may be included in a survey or other type of correspondence):

- What was the most difficult or frustrating part of the process?
- What were some positive aspects of responding to user queries?
- What do you wish you knew before answering these test questions?
- What did you learn from participating in the process?

In addition to questioning experts during the pilot test, it is also helpful to obtain feedback from participating **users**. If users are young children, it may be necessary to ask a teacher or parent for feedback. Questions may include the following:

- Were you happy or unhappy with your response?
- Did you receive the type of answer you expected?
- What other type of information do you wish the expert included in the message?
- Would you use the service again?

4.3 Scaling Up

Revision: Turning Pilot Results Into Action

Once the pilot test has been conducted and results gathered and analyzed, the service may identify areas for revision and further development. Table 4-2 shows an example of a set of results and possible actions during revision.

Table 4-2 Example of Pilot Test Results and Corresponding Actions

Results and Feedback	Actions
1. Too many rules to remember in terms of required response components.	1. Create checklist for information specialists to refer to when composing responses.
2. Takes longer than suggested time to create response.	2. Extend required turnaround time (two school days as opposed to one school day).
3. Confusion regarding the type of answer to provide (factual answer vs. pointer to resources).	3. Revise policy regarding nature of response and goals of service (include set of information resources in each response unless question requires simple answer).
4. Some participants encountered criticism from peers: that virtual experts were replacing school-based professionals and resources.	4. Change in policy to reflect that all responses must include a reference back to the students' school resources (library media specialist, teachers, print and electronic resources) as appropriate.
5. Need additional information from users in order to write appropriate response.	5. Revise policy to allow volunteers to respond to user to gather more detailed information; include fields on query form asking students to include information along with question (grade level, assignment, subject, etc.).

Making the Transition From Prototype to Contributing Service

If pilot test results indicate the need for large-scale change, the service may begin a new prototyping phase and subsequent pilot test. Some services may conduct several pilot tests before they are ready to offer the service to the public. The appropriate time for transition depends on the individual service's resources, experience, and to some extent, willingness to take a risk.

In any case, the transition from prototype to "live" service should be a gradual one. As previously discussed, AskA services experience development and change on a continual basis. After a successful pilot test, the service can gradually add staff, users, and other service components as resources and experiences allow. Once a service is in its next "Contributing" stage, it will have the opportunity for constant evaluation and revision over time (see Module 6: Evaluating).

Module 4 Summary

This section provided information, suggestions, and examples for creating a prototype of an AskA service and conducting a pilot test.

- Prototypes of AskA services are representations of the ultimate service that allow organizations to simulate service in a controlled environment while utilizing the least amount of resources. Some services experience this stage as a natural starting point; others make a distinct effort to conduct a formal test before the service is made public.

- Organizations can manipulate AskA plans to create a prototype by:
    1. Controlling the group of experts or information specialists
    2. Controlling the user audience
    3. Limiting advertising to professional outlets (stressing awareness of service)
    4. Utilizing available technology (rather than waiting for the perfect solution).

- Pilot tests are conducted to test the prototype and should
    1. Maintain control of time, activities, and objectives
    2. Provide opportunities for communication between all participants and service administrators.

- Depending on pilot test objectives, questions and discussion can address question-answer policy and procedure, comfort level of participants in conducting job functions, and user satisfaction.

- Pilot test results should lead naturally to revision of the prototype. Revision activities may include resource creation and revision of policies and procedures.

- Using the revised prototype, organizations can transition smoothly into active service, or the Contributing stage (see Module 5).

Pilot Testing the KidsConnect Service

by Blythe Bennett

About KidsConnect

General Information

KidsConnect is a question answering, help, and referral service for K–12 students on the Internet. KidsConnect is one of five components of the ICONnect Technology Initiative from the American Association of School Librarians (AASL), a division of the American Library Association (ALA). KidsConnect receives its funding from Microsoft Corporation. The service is maintained by a KidsConnect coordinator who works at the Information Institute of Syracuse, the organization that also operates the AskERIC service. School library media specialists from around the world volunteer to assist students looking for resources for school projects and assignments. All volunteers participate in a training session facilitated by a KidsConnect trainer; trainees read the service manual and must successfully complete a series of practice questions before taking on actual student questions.

History

KidsConnect began in July 1995 as a project of AASL through their ICONnect initiative. A KidsConnect coordinator was hired in July 1995 to begin the initial planning stages. The coordinator participated as an AskERIC question-answer specialist to learn the procedure of an Internet-based question-and-answer service. During the time of the coordinator's own training, a group of pilot test volunteers were enlisted and offered input as to procedure and policy of the service, and volunteer training materials were prepared. All this planning took place via e-mail among people who had not met each other in person (for the most part). Pilot testing began in November 1995, and there were four series of tests and debriefing sessions all conducted via e-mail. The pilot stages ended in March 1996, and the service launched in mid-April 1996 as part of the ALA Library Week activities.

Implementing the Pilot Test

Purpose for Pilot Test

The pilot testing was conducted for several reasons. First, it gave the volunteer media specialists the opportunity to practice the procedure for responding to student questions. These people were already skilled school librarians, but they needed the practice of doing their usual job with the e-mail interface rather than working face to face with their students. Second, the pilot sessions also allowed the KidsConnect coordinator to practice the sorting and routing system that would best fit the service and technological capabilities available. Also, some unexpected benefits surfaced. For example, some issues came up as a result of the pilot testing that were useful in making policy decisions that currently drive the project.

Such decisions made during the pilot test included these:

1. KidsConnect will not serve as a fax or interlibrary loan service.
2. KidsConnect responses will not provide direct answers to students but rather pointers to resources where an answer can be found.

Pilot Test Organization

Participants of the pilot sessions were solicited from the school media listserv, LM_NET (*http://ericir.syr.edu/lm_net*). Participants had to be school librarians who were also members of AASL. Ten volunteers in the United States agreed to be a part of the first pilot session, the initial training and feedback team. It is interesting to note that of those first 10 people, nine are *still* with the project, three years later. These people conversed via e-mail for several months while the beginning stages of the training manual were written and tested by the coordinator. In November 1995, this first group of 10 volunteers all completed a series of responses to practice questions; the coordinator then provided feedback on each response. Formative feedback was given after each practice question before any further questions were sent so the volunteer could learn what was correctly done with a response and what needed to be improved.

After this initial week of practice, there was a debriefing session that allowed the volunteers to say what worked for them and what proved most difficult. The main drawback expressed was the time it took to respond to the questions. All the volunteers were in their own schools with their own jobs to conduct, so finding time to respond to questions was the major problem they encountered. Prior to this pilot test, it was thought that volunteers would be requested to take no more than two questions a day, but this was changed to no more than one question per day, a policy that still is in effect.

The second pilot test session was much the same as the first, but with a slightly larger group of participants. Five new participants were added to the original 10 to form the second pilot group of 15 people starting in January 1996. The third pilot test took place in February 1996 with 20 participants, and the final test took place in March 1996 with 30 volunteers. Each pilot group built on the previous one, so the "veteran" volunteers became more comfortable and faster with composing their responses. Again, all participants communicated via e-mail, and most never met in person but began to build a virtual community of volunteers. This aspect of community is a key component of today's service; the volunteers feel a sense of belonging to a group working toward a common goal, although the relationships are mostly virtual.

Pilot Test Challenges and Lessons Learned

The main problem encountered during the pilot tests was the fact that the coordinator was using much faster technology than the participating library media specialists. Originally, the coordinator was not aware of the longer search time required by school librarians in typical schools with lower end technology. Participants usually found it difficult to research and compose a response in the suggested 10–15-minute time period; on many occasions it took participants generally double the time. As volunteers got more experienced with the way to respond and also with their own searching skills, they did take less time, but still not as short a time as we hoped. One other area we could have developed more before launching the service was to set more policy issues; however, some issues didn't arise until the service was underway and the policies were established.

Using Results of Pilot Test

The service operates today much the way it was intended, but with some minor changes. For instance, volunteers are not expected to answer more than one question per day, and training has been refined and improved over the first year based on feedback from the trainees.

There were some unexpected benefits for the volunteers as a result of participating in the service that are interesting to note. For instance, volunteers have indicated gaining a sense of accomplishment and intellectual stimulation, improvement of Internet and general reference and research skills, and the opportunity to make a positive impact on the local school community.

Transition to Public Service

The transition from pilot testing to public service was quite easy since there was no publicity and no large increase in the numbers of incoming questions. However, as a word of caution, once you do plan for publicity, you need to remember to keep one or two steps ahead of demand. Always keep adding to your volunteer base if you want the service to grow, maintain the turnaround time limits you set for the service, and be careful to avoid burnout, especially if the service operates with volunteers as opposed to paid employees.

Staff Motivation: Ensuring Success Beyond the Prototype

Any organization that relies on volunteer power must consider the benefits that volunteers can gain from participation. Although they usually do their part of the service out of a sense of professionalism or for fun, they need to benefit somehow from the many hours they put into the service. They have their own obligations at work and in their personal lives, so it is a true commitment to be a part of a volunteer organization that takes quite a bit of their time. They need to reap rewards (whether expected or unexpected) in order to help keep their commitment and enthusiasm alive. KidsConnect can offer the following advice based on experience:

- Offer positive and corrective feedback on volunteers' responses. It is important to let volunteers know that someone else has taken the time to read and comment on their responses on occasion.
- Establish a sense of a virtual community so that the volunteers feel a part of a group. This helps build their confidence in service participation as well as in their professional roles.
- Help volunteers transfer the skills and knowledge gained from the service to their own job roles.

Blythe Allison Bennett, *blythe@ericir.syr.edu*, is the KidsConnect Q and A Coordinator.

Module 5

| Informing |
| Planning |
| Training |
| Prototyping |
| **Contributing** |
| Evaluating |

Contributing

Operating and Maintaining the AskA Service

Module Profile

Once an AskA service has been tested and revised, an organization is ready to offer the service to its intended audience. This module is designed to prepare organizations to promote, manage, and maintain an AskA service. At the conclusion of this module, you will be able to achieve the following goal:

Goal   Manage service development and operations and build partnerships to gain necessary support and share processes.

Prerequisites   Before contributing as an AskA service, an organization should be able to do the following:

1. Collect information on the general digital reference field and existing AskA services (see Module 1: Informing).

2. Determine the best way to build and maintain digital reference service within the organization (see Module 2: Planning).

3. Plan, produce, implement, and manage training programs for service staff and information specialists (see Module 3: Training).

4. Create a prototype and conduct a pilot test of an AskA service (see Module 4: Prototyping).

Objectives   At the completion of this module, you will be able to achieve the following objectives:

1. Publicize service to potential users.
2. Identify strategies for handling increase in questions.
3. Create resources to support AskA service.
4. Build partnerships with other organizations to support service.
5. Recruit expert (information specialist) base.

5.1 Contributing an AskA Service: Putting It All Together

The ongoing stage of offering service to the K–12 community is referred to as "contributing." A new service can contribute to the overall collection of AskA services for the K–12 community in terms of incoming questions, expert responses, knowledge, and experience. In addition, the AskA service can contribute to its supporting organization by providing a mechanism for user feedback.

5.2 Developing and Managing Service

A contributing AskA service requires ongoing maintenance and troubleshooting and a constant eye towards revision and change. This section offers suggestions and examples for publicizing an AskA service to users, managing growing numbers of questions, and building supporting resources.

Publicity Strategies

Besides the obvious reason for publicizing an AskA service (i.e., to gain users), services should also consider publicizing as a responsibility. AskA services providing information to the K–12 community are responsible for informing potential users of the value that can be gained from use of the service. By offering this important information to the public, an AskA service makes an effort to reach K–12 communities across the country and helps to decrease the gap between the "haves" and the "have-nots" in terms of effective learning opportunities.

The extent and nature of publicity depends on the resources available to the organization. For instance, an AskA service with a large budget may consider launching a mail campaign to a large audience (e.g., to a mailing list of a professional publication or association) in order to reach potential users who might not be as likely to come across the service on the Internet. Services with smaller budgets may choose to simply register with Web search engines and negotiate with related Web sites for placement of links to the service's Web page.

A well-defined public relations plan can ensure that services are well-publicized and promoted on a regular basis. It is common practice for new services or services with limited resources to avoid publicizing opportunities for fear of increasing their numbers of questions beyond control. This is a valid concern. However, the overall publicizing plan should account for a gradual growth in numbers and resources over time. By making an effort to start slowly in the prototyping stage (by targeting a limited audience), the stage is already set for a steady growth in publicity as well as service development. Methods for publicizing a digital reference service may include the following:

Print-based and Face-to-Face Publicity

- **Target direct mail campaigns to potential users**—A snail-mailed postcard or flyer works well to introduce the AskA service to even a non–Internet-savvy audience — and may even provide them with a reason to get connected. It also guarantees service visibility among more than one audience even when the computer is turned off (e.g., postcards may travel around a school from teacher to teacher, be posted on a bulletin board, or be copied and placed in mailboxes). Mailing lists may be acquired from journal subscription lists, professional association membership lists, etc. However, this possibility is realistic only for services with large enough budgets to cover the printing and mailing costs.

- **Distribute fliers and handouts**—A less expensive option than direct mail, distributing paper-based advertisements by hand can increase the visibility of an AskA service. This possibility is appropriate for libraries and other institutions that experience "drop-ins" to a central facility or for services whose representatives attend conferences and meetings.

- **Advertise in professional or institutional publications**—Depending on the nature of the organization supporting the AskA service (as well as the resources), it may be appropriate to advertise in a professional or institutional publication (e.g., journals, newsletters, etc.).

- **Attend and present at professional conferences and meetings**—Many AskA services are well promoted at professional conferences and meetings when representatives have the opportunity to present and explain important information about the service and potential users and participants can ask questions. Besides presentation and discussion opportunities, services can also present at trade show booths as a way to capture walk-through traffic.

Internet-based Publicity

- **Post promotional messages to appropriate electronic discussion groups and listservs**—This is a good way to target audiences with specific interests (e.g., educational technology, math education, parenting issues, etc.). A posting can travel from one list member's e-mail account to that of a colleague. This is an inexpensive way (only cost is Internet connection) to advertise to a targeted audience (see Dr. Math case study).

- **Provide references to the service on related Web sites**—This requires an effort on the part of the AskA service staff to identify related sites and ask site publishers (Webmasters, etc.) to provide a link to the AskA service. Depending on the nature of the arrangement, this could entail a link or some information about the service accompanied by a link. For instance, the Virtual Reference Desk AskA+ Locator *http://www.vrd.org/locator/* provides links to and profiles of K–12-related AskA services that meet general quality criteria (see Module 1: Informing).

- **Link from Internet service provider pages**—Besides sites on the World Wide Web, services may also consider arrangements with Internet service providers whereby an AskA service is linked from a directory on a page accessed by members only. For instance, the National Museum of American Art Reference Desk has a link from America Online's "Reference and Learn Channel." This allows the service to attract people whose central (or only) point of access to the World Wide Web is through the provider (see National Museum of American Art case study).

- **Place reference to AskA service prominently on own organization's Web site**—Organizations can control the amount of exposure of their AskA service by the placement of service access on their Web site. The highest level of visibility of a service can be gained through a link at the "top" of the sponsoring Web site (i.e., the home page or one of the first Web pages accessed upon arrival to the site). For instance, AskERIC experimented by placing a colorful "banner" graphic on its home page reading, "Got an education question? AskERIC," which linked to the service's question submission form. This nearly tripled AskERIC's question load (see AskERIC case study).

- **List site with search engine**—An organization can register with major search engines (e.g., Yahoo!, Alta Vista, WebCrawler, InfoSeek, etc.) in order to ensure prominent placement of a Web page in users' search results. Completing a registration form for a particular search engine allows the AskA service representative to present key information about the AskA service in an organized manner. (For meta-guides to search engine registration, see SiteOwner *http://www.siteowner.com/* or SubmitIt *http://www.submit-it.com/*.) However, it is not necessary to register with a search engine in order for a particular site to appear during a search. Search engines pick up Web pages based on keywords. Therefore, it is important to include keywords on an AskA service's Web pages that reflect common questions or topics.

Managing Growing Numbers of Questions

If publicity attempts are successful (whether intended or not) and if your service is of value, users will catch on. As more people and classrooms become connected to the Internet, AskA services experience more and more traffic. AskERIC has seen an increase from 151 questions per week in 1992 to 868 questions per week in 1998 (see AskERIC case study). KidsConnect experienced 1000% growth during the month of September 1996 (Lankes, 1997).

It is projected that by the year 2000, there will be approximately 54 million students enrolled in elementary and secondary schools in the U.S.; 39 million in grades K–8 and 15 million in grades 9–12 (Lankes, Bry & Whitehead, 1996). The implications for AskA services may seem frightening, but services can prepare themselves for high volume using certain strategies and support mechanisms. The first step is to make a gradual transition from the prototype phase to the contributing phase (see Module 4: Prototyping). Below are some additional strategies and support mechanisms for ongoing control of question volume (also see AskERIC case study):

1. Gradually increase staff and expert base. Whether a service functions with full-time paid employees or part-time volunteer experts, most services have learned that increasing human resources is crucial in terms of managing increasing user questions. In order to address the greatest number of incoming questions, AskA services require a team of individuals dedicated to answering questions and supporting the work of those who answer questions. This team can be built over time according to the resources available and processes in place. For instance, a service may be able to add only a small number of new experts at one time, because each new participant must undergo a time-consuming training process managed by a limited number of staff members.

2. Automate processes as needed. Over time (or sometimes right away), many services discover that some manual tasks can be completed more quickly with the aid of a computer-based system. This can range from distributing a stock e-mail response informing a user that his or her or her question has been received to running an incoming question through a knowledge base to determine if a response is already in the system.

Another method of automation is to provide Internet-based resources to supplement the question-answer process (e.g., archive of questions and answers and lists of frequently asked questions; see Building Information Resources). Below are examples of original software packages developed by AskA services to automate their specific tasks:

- *Doctor's Office*—This software package written by "Math Doctor" Ken Williams lists incoming questions in a "triage area" in which information specialists select questions to answer and place answered questions and responses in a "post-op area" where responses can be checked by other staff before going out to users. The software also accommodates administrative tasks and access to resources and includes a help function (*http://forum.swarthmore.edu/dr.math/office_help/dr.office_help.html*).

- *MODERATOR*—This software from the MAD Scientist Network does several functions including formatting incoming questions to HTML; adding and modifying data in the databases of experts, etc.; maintaining statistics on expert performance; reviewing questions and answers; tracking routing of questions; and general site maintenance (*http://www.madsci.org/ask_expert/2.html*).

However, no matter how much automation is implemented, it is important to maintain a level of human intermediation. The value of AskA services is due in large part to the quality of person-to-person communication.

3. Maintain standard policies for recurring procedures and issues. Policies for question answering and other procedures not only ensure consistency and quality in responses to users (and other service resources), but help to speed up processes as well. For instance, if an expert is required to include a set of components in every response, the act of including these components in a response becomes a habit for the expert. Policies are created in the planning stage and are communicated to experts and staff during training; however, it is important to constantly reinforce policies through mechanisms such as manuals and job aids for use after formal training programs.

4. Control publicity. As previously mentioned, publicity efforts should be handled carefully so as not to generate more traffic than can be accommodated at a given time. Major publicity efforts such as large-scale mailings or prominent links on popular Web pages should be implemented only when staff (experts and support crew) and question-answer processes are prepared to address each question according to the AskA service's policies and goals.

5. Share questions and knowledge. AskA services can partner with other services and organizations to ease question loads and facilitate the question-answer process. Out-of-scope questions can be forwarded to more appropriate services, and responses generated from one AskA service can help information specialists from other services compose responses. The Virtual Reference Desk Project provides a set of resources and services to promote this type of question and knowledge sharing. The technical infrastructure allows AskA services to forward out-of-scope or overload questions to the central Virtual Reference Desk location to then be distributed to other services. (See Building Partnerships section.)

Building Information Resources

Many AskA services view resource development as a significant component of the service; others devote less time and energy to resources and more to the question-answering process. As with most decisions regarding AskA services, this one depends on time, funding, and staff of the service. Some AskA service information resources require a large amount of technical talent and financial resources, while others require basic HTML skills and access to a Web server (e.g., through sponsoring university).

Resources such as an archive of questions and answers, lists of frequently asked questions, and supplemental information serve both to facilitate the question-answer process and to reinforce important subject information for K–12 users. Decisions regarding information to be included on a service's Web site usually stem from feedback in the form of user questions and other communications. In building AskA service information resources, organizations should consider content, format, technical, and legal and ethical issues. Below are some suggestions and examples to help organizations build information resources for their AskA services.

Building and Organizing Content

As previously mentioned, AskA service Web site content is often based on user needs as identified by user questions and other forms of feedback. For a beginning service, content can reflect the general scope of the service and identified needs of the potential audience. When considering content to include, AskA service representatives should decide what information is most useful to the user and most accurately reflects the service scope. It is also helpful to consider what information would be useful for information specialists or experts in creating responses.

Organizations may want to include information that

- Dissuades users from submitting commonly asked, basic questions to the service
- Introduces users to the general subject matter
- Draws users back to the site, or
- Reflects in-scope questions (e.g., actual questions or examples of the types of questions the service would *like* to receive).

In addition to choosing relevant and helpful information, services should ensure that the information is easy for users to access. Below are some common types of information found on AskA service (and supporting organization) Web sites and examples of how information is presented:

Previously-Asked Questions and Answers. A large number of AskA services provide access to some or all user questions and corresponding responses. This type of collection is commonly referred to as an archive. Archives can be organized by topic, date answered (month and year), grade level or age of user, etc. Question-answer sets can be accessed through link indexes, search engines, or both.

Examples of searchable archives:

- **MAD Scientist Network** *http://madsci.wustl.edu/MS_search.html*—This archive is searchable by keyword. Users can select options for Boolean searching, files to search, hits per page, science area, and grade level. Results appear as lists of questions, representing either the original question or a response, accompanied by information about the person who posted the message (i.e., either the user who posted the question or the scientist who answered it). Users click on the question to link to the full-text question (which contains a link to the response) or directly to the response. (The search interface runs with Apache's mod_perl; the search script is a front end to a Glimpse server.)
- **ScienceNet Database** *http://www.sciencenet.org.uk/qpages/search.html*—The main search page allows users to select a section of the question-answer database to search (e.g., archaeology, chemistry, etc.). An option is also available to search the entire database. The database uses a Glimpse search engine.
- **How Things Work**
  http://landau1.phys.virginia.edu/Education/Teaching/HowThingsWork/qsearch.html
  —Users can search for keywords in questions or answers. Results appear as a string of full-text questions and answers.

When including a search engine on an AskA service site, it is a good idea to include a "help" section with directions for the user audience.

Examples of listed or categorized archive:

- **Ask Dr. Math** *http://forum.swarthmore.edu/dr.math/*—In addition to offering a search engine for its archive, Ask Dr. Math provides access to its questions and answers through an organized set of links. Users may choose a section of the archive based on grade level (e.g., elementary, middle school, etc.) and then topic. Links from the topic list lead to full-text question-answer sets.

- **Ask A NASA Scientist**
  http://imagine.gsfc.nasa.gov/docs/ask_astro/ask_an_astronomer.html—This site organizes its question-answer sets by topic but highlights those topics that reflect the scientists' main areas of expertise (e.g., cosmology, quasars, etc.). Thus, the topic list on the main page is divided into two categories, expertise areas and additional topics, no doubt in an attempt to encourage in-scope questions while not discouraging others. Topic lists link to question lists, which link to full-text question-answer sets.

Frequently Asked Questions and Answers. Frequently asked questions, or FAQs, are also a common feature on AskA service Web sites. The questions to highlight in an FAQ may be determined in a number of ways; this can include automated tracking of incoming question topics or observation by AskA service staff who are familiar with incoming questions. Most FAQs are categorized by topic and sometimes further broken down by subtopic. By providing FAQs, services have the opportunity to highlight exemplary, sometimes comprehensive, responses to common questions.

Examples of frequently asked questions and answers:

- **Top 101 Ask a Volcanologist Questions**
  http://volcano.und.nodak.edu/vwdocs/frequent_questions/top_101/Top_101.html—This service requires that users review the FAQs in order to gain access to the question submission form (or *any* information regarding sending a question). This forces a user to make sure that his or her question has not yet been answered so that the small team of experts can control the number of questions received.

- **Internet Public Library Frequently Asked Reference Questions (FARQ)**
  http://www.ipl.org/ref/QUE/FARQ/FARQ.html—This FARQ page presents each topic broken down into subjects; each subject name (e.g., literary criticism, genealogy) is accompanied by a sample question that can be answered by reviewing the particular FARQ. Since the Internet Public Library's AskA service offers expertise in general reference, the actual FARQ pages include some introductory information and references to other resources.

Supplemental Information. Besides offering access to question-answer sets (whether from archive or FAQs), some AskA services provide additional information and resources to supplement the knowledge generated by the question-answer process. This can include references to related sources (e.g., links to Web sites), Web pages with factual information on related topics, or complete collections of related resources for the target audience.

Examples of supplemental information resources from AskA services:

- **Ask Shamu** *http://www.seaworld.org/ask_shamu/asindex.html*—The responses in the question-answer archive include links to Web pages with detailed information and photographs on particular marine animals provided by the sponsoring organization (Sea World/Busch Gardens). For example, detailed information on killer whales is referenced in a response to the question "Can an orca whale have twins?"

- **KidsConnect Favorite Web Sites for K–12 Students** *http://www.ala.org/ICONN/kcfavorites.html*—Volunteer library media specialists from the KidsConnect services created a list of Web sites relating to topics commonly addressed in student questions (e.g., animals, geography). The list of sites was intended to aid students as well as volunteers answering questions.

- **AskERIC Virtual Library** *http://www.askeric.org/Virtual/*—AskERIC has built a comprehensive set of educational resources for educators and others interested in educational research and practice. Resources in the Virtual Library include pathfinders to information on educational topics; lesson plans; educational listserv archives; links to education-related Web sites; and links to other resources from the parent organization (Educational Resources Information Center).

AskA services constantly strive to provide better access to information to their users. For instance, Ask Dr. Math is currently looking into the possibility of automatically matching incoming questions with responses in the archive so that users are directed to relevant information before the question is further addressed by an expert or service administrator (see Dr. Math case study, Module 2: Planning).

Legal and Ethical Issues and Solutions

As discussed in Module 1: Informing, there are some legal and ethical issues to consider when providing an AskA service. These issues come into play not only in providing responses to users but in providing resources on the AskA service Web site as well. The following discussion identifies legal and ethical issues along with solutions implemented by some AskA services. In addition to the suggestions below, services may also consider obtaining legal advice regarding these issues.

User Privacy and Confidentiality. When posting question-answer sets on a public Web site (e.g., in an archive), AskA services should be careful not to provide access to information that can identify individual users in any way (see Module 1: Informing). Options for maintaining confidentiality of user information include these:

- **Stripping all identifiers from messages before posting them on the site.** For services with small numbers of incoming questions, this may be done manually (i.e., by deleting contact and other personal information from the message); for those with larger question numbers, identifying information may be stripped automatically (i.e., by programming the system to remove information in certain fields such as "name," "e-mail address," etc.).

- **Limiting access to user information.** While stripping personal information from given fields works in many cases, it is impossible to control personal information that appears in the body of users' messages. Some AskA services do not trust technology to remove identifying user information from all areas of user messages. In this case, if manual revision is not possible, the service may want to limit access to the question-answer archive to those with authority—AskA service staff and information specialists.

Many services include user information in their archive, but make efforts to discourage the use of such information for commercial purposes (e.g., mass e-mail, etc.; see MAD Scientist disclaimer *http://www.madsci.org/info/disclaimer.html*).

One way to ensure privacy during the question-answer process is to post user responses on password-protected Web pages.

Copyright. As in any content development, information on AskA service Web sites should be presented accurately, giving appropriate credit to original authors. Individuals developing content other than that based on information specialist expertise should be sure to cite when appropriate.

Another copyright issue involves services' ownership rights to information on their own sites (e.g., question-answer sets, FAQs, etc.). Many services may not own rights to their resources depending on individual service issues such as policies of sponsoring organizations (see Module 1). Those that do wish to protect their information from being used without permission (e.g., images or text downloaded for use on others' Web sites) should include a policy statement on the service Web site.

Liability. This issue applies to all AskA services to some degree but is especially important for services whose expert information can be interpreted as professional advice —medical, legal, etc. Protocol for guarding against liability in information specialists' responses should be addressed in the AskA service policy. (Solutions for communicating liability matters in responses can include creating an electronic signature with a disclaimer.) However, attention should also be paid to liability issues when creating resources for the AskA service Web site. Protecting a service against liability can be as simple as placing a disclaimer on the service's home page or question submission page.

Examples of disclaimers on AskA service Web sites include these:

- **Ask the Optometrist** *http://www.visioncare.com/ask.html*—The main page for this AskA service includes a lengthy disclaimer stating that by submitting a question, the user agrees that he or she does not become the doctor's patient, should seek care from a competent professional, and does not hold the doctor or organization liable for care.

- **MAD Scientist Network** *http://www.madsci.org/info/disclaimer.html*—This site includes a disclaimer including statements that the information on the site (as well as in responses to users) does not represent the views of the sponsoring institution or the institutions of individual experts; is for educational purposes only and should not be interpreted as medical or professional advice; and is not guaranteed to be completely accurate. (Instructions are provided for submitting corrections to errors found on the site).

Technical Support and Development

Besides selecting and creating content for the AskA service site, a service needs to plan for the technical development and upkeep of the resources. This can range from creating simple HTML files of FAQs to building a search engine for question-answer archives. (Some systems integrate resource development and access capabilities with overall automation of the question-answer process such as question routing, etc. See "Managing Growing Numbers of Questions.")

For a detailed guide to software and systems for AskA services, refer to the MAD Scientist Network's "Setting Up an Ask-An-Expert Service," Section VI *http://www.madsci.org/ask_expert/6.html* (Bry, 1997). Descriptions and suggestions are provided for Web servers, operating systems, mail programs, search engines, and interactive communications tools for service administrators and information specialists. Information on product quality and cost is included.

5.3 Building Partnerships

Individual K–12 AskA services are not alone in their goal to provide quality information to the education community. AskA services, businesses, professional associations, government agencies, educational institutions, and other bodies can work together to support various facets of AskA service: software, Web space, expert (information specialist) recruiting, publicizing, etc. AskA services can seek support through the Virtual Reference Desk Project as well as other associations promoting similar interests and goals.

The Virtual Reference Desk Project

The Virtual Reference Desk Project is developing a set of resources and services to assist AskA services in managing their question-answer process. Specific components of the Project include the following:

1. AskA Consortium. The AskA Consortium is a network of organizations in areas of technology, digital reference, library science, business, and education to help guide the Virtual Reference Desk Project and develop necessary resources and support. Included in the AskA Consortium are AskA services that agree to adhere to quality criteria as identified by the Virtual Reference Desk (see Module 1: Informing). AskA services in the Consortium will participate in a process of question sharing and contribute question-answer sets to the Knowledge Base (see below).

2. Meta-Triage Function. The meta-triage is the central switchboard for questions and answers traversing the Virtual Reference Desk's network of users and knowledge resources. The meta-triage function takes questions from the K–12 community directly as well as from the AskA services in the AskA Consortium. In this way if an AskA service receives too many questions, overload questions can be routed to other AskA services that are underutilized. An AskA service can also send a question to the meta-triage function if it does not match the expertise provided by that AskA service. In this way if an AskA service receives a question from a user and is unable to answer it (a science question sent to a math service, for example), it can use the meta-triage to get the user's question to the best knowledge resource.

3. Knowledge Base. The Knowledge Base represents a structured collection of existing question-answer sets. It is distributed with its contents managed by the varying AskA services. The knowledge base can help AskA services manage an increase in questions by providing a resource for users to consult prior to question submission and can help experts by providing information that can be used to compose responses. While individual AskA services may have their own knowledge bases (or "archive"), the Virtual Reference Desk Knowledge Base provides a more comprehensive set of resources from all AskA services in the Consortium.

Membership in Associations

Partnering with professional associations can offer many benefits to AskA services. Some services have in fact grown out of professional associations (e.g., KidsConnect is part of an initiative of the American Association of School Librarians [AASL], a division of the American Library Association [ALA]). These services are more likely to start out with built-in expert and user bases.

There are different models of working with a professional association:

Association ownership. In this model the association owns and operates the service. While outside contractors or experts may aid in the logistics of the service, it is the association's ownership that drives the service. Associations can use an AskA service to provide increased training and development opportunities to its members, increase visibility inside or outside its community, create a direct method for taking information from its users or community (through the questions they ask), or promote an agenda to a larger community (such as the importance of topic X in the K–12 curriculum). Several AskA services were created to fill perceived gaps in K–12 curricula (e.g., art education). AskA services benefit from such arrangements when associations allow the service access to user communities that have already been identified. For instance KidsConnect promotion could coincide with AASL's promotion of reading in the schools and ALA's promotion of public library use. In this case, the association provided access to its own users and its target populations through traditional promotion techniques such as mailers. In addition, associations can provide links to their partner AskA services from their home page, which could boost question numbers from appropriate users.

Association expert base. In this model the AskA service is run by a service or organization external to an association. The association and external organizational mission are at the very least aligned, but the association does not take on the longer term funding and operational concerns. The association instead promotes the AskA service internally to its members as a way of seeking volunteers to work with the external AskA service. The association gains outreach and achieves mission objectives without the burden of AskA service support and funding. Members of professional associations often reflect the most dedicated and talented representatives of a particular field. By offering its membership base as a possible information specialist pool, an association not only provides the K–12 community with needed expertise but also offers meaningful volunteer and professional development experiences for its members. Benefits of participating in digital reference services include improvement of general skills (e.g., Internet searching, subject knowledge) and personal satisfaction of helping users solve information problems.

Association sponsorship. This model requires the least commitment and resources by an association. The association becomes a promoter or resource provider to an AskA service without direct involvement in the day-to-day operations. The association acts as a sort of "seal-of-approval" agency to the AskA service.

While these models reflect how associations can become involved in AskA services (particularly K–12 AskA services), they do not directly address why associations should consider becoming involved.

Such a discussion must ultimately align to the mission and membership of the organization, but the following is an initial list of reasons professional associations should consider creating, participating in, or sponsoring an AskA service:

- **Membership outreach.** Association can use the AskA service as a means to increase participation by its members. Answering questions requires less involvement than committee work and can be infinitely more rewarding.

- **Membership training.** AskA services can provide a concrete and directed opportunity to increase the skill sets of an association's membership. This training can be in topical areas associated with the organization, Internet skills, communications skills, etc. (see Module 3: Training). For example if members are going to be answering questions on topic x, they may be expected to have a certain level of understanding of that topic. This may lead to the creation of standards and certification processes in this topic.

- **Increased attention to association issues by a given community.** Associations by definition have an agenda. By providing an easy-to-use and credible service to a targeted community rather than static resources (i.e., Web pages), an association can become a preferred source of information on a given topic. As a preferred source, the association can further its agenda while meeting people's information needs.

- **Increased visibility of the association.** By answering the questions of a larger community, such as the K–12 education community, an association can send its message and create an identity beyond its membership.

- **Recruitment of members.** With increased visibility and participation opportunities, association membership can increase. For example, AskA services can send a short invitation to join an organization with every answer.

- **Highlighting association products and services.** Answers given will most likely come from ready and reliable sources. By pointing users to existing association publications, sales of association products can increase.

Professional associations have a great deal to gain in the creation of AskA services. They can use the Internet to have greater access to user and member communities than ever before. Through participation in AskA services, association members can promote important information to the public, improve skills and knowledge, and experience personal rewards that come from satisfying the information needs of the K-12 community and other Internet users.

Module 5 Summary

This section provided information, suggestions, and examples for managing AskA service development and operations and building partnerships.

- Organizations can develop and manage an AskA service through publicizing service to users, controlling growing numbers of questions, and building supporting information resources.

  1. Publicizing strategies for AskA services include print-based, face-to-face, and Internet-based methods to inform potential users of benefits gained from using the service.

  2. It is possible to manage growing numbers of questions by gradually increasing staff and information specialist base, automating processes, maintaining standard policies, controlling publicity, and sharing questions and knowledge with other services and organizations.

  3. Issues in building supporting information resources for AskA services include building and organizing content (e.g., archive, frequently asked questions, supplementary information); considering legal and ethical issues in providing access to information (e.g., privacy, copyright, liability); and planning for technical development and support.

- AskA services can build partnerships with organizations, associations, and other services in order to balance question loads, recruit information specialists, and build user base.

  1. The Virtual Reference Desk Project provides resources and services to help AskA services share out-of-scope and overload questions and access question-answer sets from other services.

  2. Partnering with professional associations provides many benefits to both AskA service and associations (e.g., association members who serve as information specialists provide important expertise to the K–12 community while gaining professional development experience).

167

Case Studies in Contributing

The following case studies from representatives of existing AskA services provide real-life stories about managing and operating an AskA service.

- *Hosting Ask the Space Scientist:* Dr. Sten Odenwald describes success factors and indicators of NASA's Ask the Astronomer and Ask the Space Scientist services and discusses issues for the future of these and other services.

- *Managing Growing Numbers for AskERIC*: Coordinator Pauline Lynch shares AskERIC's strategies for managing a growth in questions from 151 to 868 per week.

Hosting "Ask the Space Scientist"

by Dr. Sten Odenwald

The Astronomy Cafe (*http://www2.ari.net/home/odenwald/cafe.html*) offers access to many documents about research in astronomy as well as the Ask the Astronomer (ATA) service (*http://image.gsfc.nasa.gov/poetry/astro/qanda.html*). A similar site, Ask the Space Scientist (ATSS) (*http://http:www2.ari.net/home/odenwald/qadir/qanda.html*), was developed for the NASA IMAGE satellite program as part of their Education and Public Outreach service (residing on the IMAGE/POETRY site: *http://image.gsfc.nasa.gov/poetry/*). Following 32 months of operation at the Astronomy Cafe and 12 months at the IMAGE/POETRY site, over 4500 questions have been logged and answered at ATA and ATSS at a rate of about 30-50 per week day. Since detailed monthly statistics of site activity are automatically recorded, it is possible to analyze some of the parameters of the ATA/ATSS service that seem to affect its success and to anticipate changes in service and site management for the future.

Success Factors and Indicators

Shortage of Quality Astronomy-Related AskA Services

Currently, there is a shortage of astronomy-related AskA services that actively answer user questions. Among astronomy-related Web sites, some are unresponsive with a static compliment of questions, others invite visitors to pose questions, and still others are unreachable due to invalid Web addresses. Of those that solicit questions from visitors, few archive the questions and answers for the benefit of subsequent visitors.

There are some notable differences between ATA/ATSS and many of the other on-line astronomy services. At ATA/ATSS:

1. Both the question and the answer are archived and hyperlinked to several master topic indexes
2. All questions are answered no matter the level of seriousness, and an effort is made to respond to questions within a 3-4 day time period
3. There are very few large image files that take prohibitively long times to download (moreover, the text files are usually no longer than 5000 bytes in length), and
4. ATA/ATSS is maintained by a single astronomer rather than by a group. This streamlines the logistics of responding to questions, and insures that answers are not over-specialized.

Active Advertising of the Site

It is important to advertise a site adequately so that a wide enough audience is aware of it when searching for information on the Internet. The Cafe launched its advertising campaign on August 7, 1995, when its address was announced to the Netscape and National Center for Supercomputing Application (NCSA's) "What's New" pages and with the popular Yahoo (*http://www.yahoo.com*) and Infoseek (*http://www.infoseek.com*) indexes. By August 29, the Astronomy Cafe was formally added to these services. On September 1, the first few questions to ATA were received, and on September 4, NSCA selected the Cafe as the Pick of the Week. This gave a favorable review of the site, and most importantly, the NCSA review included an embedded link directly to the Cafe. This event produced a large initial increase in visitors to the site.

Following this initial recognition, the Cafe received several additional awards and reviews in the next eight months including:

-   The "Computer Wise" television program carried a review of the site on its September 20 program
-   Point Communications awarded the site its "Top 5 %" of the Internet award
-   The "Netsurfer's Digest" (*http://www.netsurf.com/nsd/*) gave the site very enthusiastic reviews as well as another embedded link from their review page
-   The McKinley Group awarded the Cafe a "3-star" rating
-   Sky and Telescope (*http://www.skypub.com*) added the Cafe to its home page as its only link to an external site, and
-   New Scientist reviewed the Cafe at its "Planet Internet" site (*http://www.newscientist.com/ps/daily/site.html*) and awarded it the "Best Site of the Day."

Maintaining a Comfortable Level of Service

In terms of advertising ATA and ATSS to interested parties on the Internet, this process has now reached close to its maximum spread and visibility. However, in paraphrasing a familiar adage, "No successful Web site will go unpunished," it is possible to become too well known. With literally millions of potential visitors, the penalty for success is that the ATA/ATSS service can be easily inundated with questions beyond the capacity of the site to service in a timely manner. The initial traffic rate in August 1995 was about 1-2 questions per day. This was a very comfortable pace handled by a single astronomer working a few hours a week. Once the ATA/ATSS sites became better known, a rate between 30-50 questions per day became common during the Monday-Friday period; this pace requires a more serious load on the astronomer, averaging about 1-2 hours per day. When designing such services for the Internet, some serious consideration must, therefore, be given to adequately staffing the site against the contingency of its own success.

Site Statistics

Statistics for ATA/ATSS show that these services are reasonably popular. The statistics show a steady increase in traffic; following an initial three month start-up phase, the percentage of site visitors who read or post questions has leveled off at about 60%. The remaining traffic goes to the other areas of the Cafe and IMAGE/POETRY Web sites.

Overall, there has been a steady increase in both the number of documents examined by site visitors and in the percentage of visitors who ask questions. Currently, one out of 30 visitors actually asks a question, and the Cafe and IMAGE/POETRY sites attract about 3600 visitors per month.

Site Improvements and The Future

Increase in Users

Dern (1996) declares that for the next few years, the capacity and services of the Internet will continue to increase and improve as new technologies are brought to bare on the problems of improved packet switching times and bandwidth. For at least the next few years, the doubling time of new Internet users is expected to remain near 12-14 months, leading to more than 100 million computers connected to the Internet by the end of the decade (Herbst, 1995). This means that the potential audience for any Ask the Astronomer activity is truly astronomical.

The experience of offering the particular Ask the Astronomer service described in this case study indicates that a similar growth trend may be present among the visitors to the Cafe and IMAGE/POETRY sites. In terms of education opportunities, it is heartening that this kind of service has not yet reached a plateau. By the same token, it is troubling that the level of effort now required to handle 40-50 questions per day by a single astronomer will not suffice to handle an additional doubling of the site activity without seriously affecting the style and content of the present resource.

Advances in Technology

In addition to the potential increase in users, there is an inevitable growth of software and hardware technology that applies pressure to developers of Web sites. Some sites have for several years incorporated limited CGI forms-based interactivity which allows visitors to enter data into document fields and submit the document for processing at the host's machine. Since the inception of the Cafe and IMAGE/POETRY sites, which were written in HTML v1.1, powerful browsers such as Microsoft's Explorer 3.0 and Netscape's Navigator 3.0 have also come into increasing usage; these browsers can handle HTML v2.02 with its extended capacity for multiple fonts, colors and table design. In addition, Sun Microsystems' Java language allows small animation programs to be downloaded along with a Web page and automatically run on the visitor's computer as "applets." HTML 3.0, which now appears at an increasing number of sites, includes equation typesetting.

172

Future Ideas and Challenges

It is easy to imagine an ATA/ATSS site utilizing many of these innovations; for example, the site could include an animation of the moon orbiting the earth while the text portion of the document describes the origin of the lunar phases. Even the evolution of the sun during the next 6 billion years could be attempted in a series of sequenced static images showing its evolution off the main sequence.

Currently, the penalty paid for implementing these increasingly elaborate options is the increase in download time, requiring that users have faster modems. A purely text-based Ask the Astronomer site, on the other hand, may download quickly but lack the visual appeal. Most K-12 schools continue to have relatively low-end technology (e.g., low-quality modems below 14,400 baud), and do not have the time during classroom hours to download elaborate graphics, clickable image maps and animations. Other visitors may have high-end systems and even T1 data lines.

Because of the technology options and the discrepancies in user technical capabilities, it is important to consider the visitor you are trying to serve. Although the current ATA/ATSS site was intended for use by the K-12 and educational communities, it is very clear from the statistics that it is not this community that is using the ATA/ATSS resources the most. This means that there is, in fact, an opportunity to further develop the Ask the Astronomy resources to match the typically high-end resources than many visitors in the .COM domain have available to them.

Developing Resources

The current generation of Ask the Astronomer sites are largely text-based. Future ideas include local topic search engines, and an increasing array of embedded images, tables, line drawings and simple animations. Some pages may even foster visitor interaction by prompting for input parameters and displaying resultant calculations allowing the visitor to perform simple numerical experiments. The biggest challenge to designers of Ask the Astronomer sites will be to keep the resources active and responsive to the diverse needs of the Internet community. Sites that provide a new experience to the visitor each time they stop by can become addictive and generate a large cadre of returning visitors. These sites will also be time consuming to update on a daily or weekly basis in response to new inquiries. It takes time to put together an elaborate HTML document with embedded graphics and animation. More importantly, increasing the graphics load of ATA/ATSS sites increases their download times and this may not be acceptable to many 'low-end' users, particularly in the K-12 area.

For the foreseeable future, text-rich ATA/ATSS sites will continue to be the mainstream offering by astronomers willing to host such sites for the public. Enhanced sites with animation and complex graphics will probably remain impractical except, perhaps, as an occasional adjunct to the answers of a small number of questions.

Dr. Sten Odenwald, *odenwald@bolero.gsfc.nasa.gov*, is the Chief Scientist with Raytheon STX Corporation and is the Public Outreach Manager for the NASA IMAGE Satellite Program.

Managing Growing Numbers of Questions for AskERIC

by Pauline Lynch

Introduction

AskERIC, the question-answer service of the Educational Resources Information Center (ERIC), provides education information to teachers, librarians, counselors, administrators, parents, and others. AskERIC began in 1992 and has since seen an increase from 151 questions per week to 868 questions per week. The service has responded to this overwhelming growth in questions by increasing staff, improving processes and tools, standardizing responses to users, and experimenting with publicity strategies.

Increasing Staff

AskERIC began with a staff of two in 1992 and has expanded gradually to over 50 staff members in 1998. A core group of general information specialists are based in the central AskERIC office at the ERIC Clearinghouse on Information and Technology. In addition to being answered by this group, questions are answered by subject experts from many of the other 15 ERIC Clearinghouses (including Elementary and Early Childhood Education; Reading, English, and Communication; and Science, Mathematics, and Environmental Education) as well as by experts from outside organizations such as the Smithsonian Institution. The decision to distribute questions outside of the central office was not based only on the sheer number of questions but also on the wide range of question topics, many of which required the expertise of subject specialists.

Improving Q&A Processes and Tools

Since user questions are routed to several places, we had to create a system to keep track of questions and responses. Early on, we began an archiving system in the form of e-mail accounts; each clearinghouse carbon copies its responses to one of the accounts. This serves as a way to archive responses according to the responding team as well as provide access to responses for quality checks by the AskERIC central staff.

As we continue to grow, we find that this manual system of tracking questions is extremely time consuming. Aside from recording which clearinghouse or individual the question is assigned to, we also keep track of the month the question was answered. While we are currently able to search the archive accounts for previously written responses by date, subject line, or e-mail, we still lack a central location to store all question-answer pairs. For this reason, we are currently in the process of implementing a new automation system that will maintain a full record of all question-answer pairs in one location and will help us record electronically the individual or clearinghouse to which a question is routed and track whether or not it has been answered.

Standardizing Responses

In 1994, we developed the *AskERIC System-Wide Guide*, a question-answer manual for all AskERIC questions. Originally, question-answer policy was unwritten, and we gave clearinghouses a lot of freedom to answer questions using their own style. Gradually we realized that the wide variety of formats for providing information was confusing users. For instance, when parts were missing or formats were changed we started to receive questions from users saying they received only a partial answer or that they did not understand what was sent. The *System-Wide Guide* still allows for personalization but within a uniform framework. For example, the guide includes a set of standard response templates for different situations (e.g., nature of question, type of resources used to answer question, etc.), but respondents are encouraged to modify any standard statements based on the specific situation.

Publicity Strategies

Publicizing the AskERIC service is extremely new for us. Until last year we advertised the service by exhibiting and presenting at national and local education-related conferences. In 1997, we found that the number of questions paralleled the previous year rather than having increased; we began to brainstorm ways to advertise the service. We found that announcements on listservs did not draw much traffic, but placing a banner on various pages of our Web site nearly tripled our question load. Since our staff was unable to keep up with this level of demand, the banners—reading "Got an Education Question? AskERIC"—were taken down after a couple of days. At the same time, we began including AskERIC promotional materials in all orders sent out from the ERIC Clearinghouse on Information and Technology (e.g., books, digests, etc.). This seems to have continued the trend but at a much more manageable level (20% more questions per week).

Conclusion

While a constant increase in questions affords many challenges and changes, it is a sign that our service is valuable to the education community. The effects of publicity are very difficult to control and may cause sudden increases in questions. Be sure to have a solid organizational structure before you look for ways to increase the question load. We learned over the past five years that starting out small and gradually increasing our staff and question load over a period of time seems to work best.

Pauline Lynch, *pauline@askeric.org*, is Coordinator for AskERIC.

Module 6

Informing
Planning
Training
Prototyping
Contributing
Evaluating

Evaluating

Measuring Effectiveness and Efficiency of AskA Services

Module Profile

Like any type of reference service, AskA services should be evaluated regularly in order to ensure quality improvement and to justify overall efforts of the service. At the conclusion of this module, you will be able to achieve the following goal:

Goal   Plan and implement evaluation of an AskA service and use results to improve service.

Prerequisites   Before evaluating an AskA service, an organization should be able to

1. Collect information on the general digital reference field and existing AskA services (see Module 1: Informing).

2. Determine the best way to build and maintain digital reference service within the organization (see Module 2: Planning).

3. Plan, produce, implement, and manage training programs for service staff and information specialists (see Module 3: Training).

4. Create a prototype and conduct a pilot test of an AskA service (see Module 4: Prototyping).

5. Manage service development and operations and build partnerships to gain necessary support and share processes (see Module 5: Contributing).

Objectives   At the completion of this module, you will be able to achieve the following objectives:

1. Understand the importance and purpose of evaluating an AskA service.
2. Identify areas of the service to be evaluated.
3. Identify standards by which to judge quality of service.
4. Identify methods for obtaining information to evaluate an AskA service.
5. State issues involved in planning an evaluation for an AskA service and applying results.

6.1 Evaluating AskA Services

The field of digital reference introduces new aspects of reference service evaluation: assessing the quality of digital question-answer transactions and reference resources from a distance. Digital reference services can learn from the research and implementation of traditional library reference evaluation—in the context of both large-scale and individual site studies.

From 1965 to 1993, over 59 studies were conducted to test the quality of reference services (Saxton, 1997).[24] Most of these studies focused on the accuracy of responses (Saxton, 1997), while there has been some emphasis on other issues, such as user satisfaction, quality of reference interview process, and individual reference librarian performance.

Digital reference evaluation can focus on some of the same issues, but they are translated into different terms: quality of information specialists' responses, user satisfaction with responses and question-answer process, and information specialist satisfaction with response process and other service policies and procedures. In addition, reference service in a virtual context implies differences in quality criteria, applications of research methods, target audiences, etc.

This section discusses the purposes for digital reference evaluation and possible areas to be evaluated. Comparisons to traditional library reference evaluation issues and techniques are included as appropriate. Emphasis is not on quality criteria for digital reference. Discussion of quality characteristics can be found in Module 1: Informing ("Facets of Quality for K–12 Digital Reference Services").

Purpose of Digital Reference Evaluation

The primary reason for conducting formal evaluation of AskA services is to ensure that goals of the service and organization are being met most efficiently and effectively. It is very easy to get caught up in the daily operations of question answering, resource building, expert recruiting, etc. and to take for granted that the service is adequately meeting user needs and is being conducted in the most cost- and resource-efficient manner. In fact, many services do not conduct formal evaluations but rather rely on other channels (detectors) including user feedback or sponsor requests to guide decision making.

---

[24] For a list of reference service evaluation studies in chronological order by date of study from 1965-1993, see Saxton (1997), pages 283-288.

This module discusses evaluation in a different context from evaluation in the Prototype phase (Module 4). The pilot test is conducted solely as a *formative* evaluation effort, meaning that the primary objective is to improve or revise service. The purpose of the Prototyping stage is to test and revise service before it operates according to its intended plan. This module discusses both *formative* and *summative* evaluation methods that can be conducted on an ongoing basis once the service is in full Contributing mode (see Module 5: Contributing).

In this context, formative evaluation efforts focus on issues of improvement (e.g., *How* can the service more effectively meet user needs? *How* can training methods be revised to better prepare information specialists for necessary tasks?), and summative evaluation efforts focus on some measurement of quality (e.g., *To what extent* is the service achieving its goals? *To what extent is* the service making the best use of its resources?). Results of summative evaluation efforts are used primarily by decision-makers to make "go/no go" decisions regarding the service (e.g., renewal of funding). Major questions asked may include these: Is the service effective in providing information to users? Is the service consistent with original goals? Does the service accommodate user needs?

Since the concept of digital reference is so new, there is not much information available in terms of best practice for evaluation of digital reference and AskA services. However, AskA services can learn a great deal from research and literature in library reference evaluation. In fact, reasons for evaluating AskA services are similar to reasons for evaluating traditional reference services. Allen (1995, pp. 208–9) presents three basic motives for evaluating reference, which can be summarized in the following list:

1. Improve services to users
2. Improve processes (efficiency)
3. Justify benefits of service to decision-makers (e.g., funders).

More specific motivations for evaluating traditional reference as well as digital reference can include these:

*   Low rate of questions are answered
*   Responses are incorrect or substandard according to service policy
*   Sponsor demands a proposal or report in order to make a funding decision
*   Users indicate dissatisfaction with responses or other aspects of service
*   Staff show signs of burnout.

Problems requiring evaluation are not always obvious; services should examine various areas of service in order to identify priorities for evaluation. The next section, "What Should Be Evaluated?" discusses possible priority areas.

What Should Be Evaluated?

As in traditional library reference, digital reference is made up of many interrelated components. These components are outlined in Module 2 as detectors, rules, and effectors. After a set of areas has been identified for evaluation, it is necessary for a particular service to prioritize the areas and select those with the highest priorities for immediate evaluation. Table 6-1 outlines areas of service to be evaluated based on possible AskA service detectors, rules, and effectors. Some areas overlap across different components and subcomponents.

Table 6-1: AskA Service Structure and Possible Areas for Evaluation

Component	Agent/Subcomponent	Sample Areas
Detectors	Users	• User characteristics and demographics • User technical capabilities • User information needs (e.g., short factual information vs. problem-solving guidance) • Users' special needs that can affect service • Satisfaction with responses (in terms of appropriateness, completeness, tone of information specialists, etc.) • Satisfaction with Internet information resources created or organized by service (type, format, content, usability) • Awareness of scope and limitations of service • Benefits gained from using service (save time, money, etc.) • Activities performed upon receiving response (e.g., information used for general interest, for school report, shared with colleagues, etc.) • Nature of user questions • Number of user questions
Rules	Process	• Cost effectiveness of systems (e.g., software), staff, procedures, etc. • Consistency with advertised turnaround time • Efficiency of technology used for triage • Number of steps taken for triage
	Resources—Policy	• Practicality of turnaround time • Appropriateness of service scope in terms of meeting user needs • Ability to restrict public access to private user information (in archived responses, etc.)

Component	Agent/Subcomponent	Sample Areas
	Resources— Information Specialists (IS)	• User perceptions of IS • IS performance (based on required skills as result of training program; e.g., accuracy in answering questions, inclusion of required response components, etc.) • Extent of burnout (lack of motivation) • General attitude towards users • Increase in skills as result of participation in service
	Resources—Tools	• Effectiveness of software for triage, question answering, and archiving
Effectors	Responses	• Extent to which responses satisfy user questions • User satisfaction with amount of information provided in response • Helpfulness of specific response components • Readability • Comprehensibility • Ability to provide users with follow-through strategies
	Supporting Information Resources	• Readability • Ability to meet user needs as identified by incoming questions • Extent to which user privacy is maintained (e.g., archive, etc.)

As the table implies, evaluation of digital reference service can cover more than the actual question-answer process. Attention can also focus on supporting information resources (e.g., archive, FAQs), personnel performance, and methods for gathering information in order to improve service.

The items above imply assessment for both effectiveness and efficiency of the service. Effectiveness is measured by looking at how well the service achieves identified goals and objectives (Hernon & McClure, 1987). For example, the achievement of service goals and objectives can be reflected by user satisfaction and response accuracy. Efficiency is measured by amount of resources involved (or costs) in achieving identified objectives (Scriven, 1991). This can include the cost of software and the time taken to conduct triage process.

Question of Quantity

Another issue that is often measured by both digital reference and traditional reference services and can be related to both effectiveness and efficiency is that of quantity: How many questions are answered by the service? How many users are visiting the service Web site?

<u>Percentage of Questions Answered</u>

The percentage of questions answered by a digital reference service relates to the criteria of *extensiveness* (Hernon & McClure, 1987) or "how much of a service is provided" (p. 1). In traditional reference service, this can be measured against the number of people served by a particular library. In digital reference service where users are potentially scattered across the globe, extensiveness is measured by the percentage of incoming questions answered. Since quantity is easily measured electronically, many services keep some ongoing statistics regarding numbers of questions received, answered, etc. However, it is important that the information obtained and recorded be used appropriately—in other words, quality should not be assumed based on any such measurement of quantity.

Specific questions that may be of interest to AskA services include these:
- How many questions come into the system per day, week, month, etc.?
- How many questions are routed to (or selected by) experts per day, week, month, etc.?
- How many questions are answered by information specialists?

Such measurements of quantity indicate a service's ability to respond to users' information needs. The Virtual Reference Desk does not consider number of questions answered in its discussion of "Facets of Quality for K–12 Digital Reference Services" because of differences in service capacities and available resources. For this reason, measurements of quantity do not necessarily indicate service quality (in addition, quantity cannot be used to measure other indications of quality such as response accuracy, inclusion of necessary components, etc.). However, if a specific question-answer rate is indicated in service goals and objectives, then quantity could be used to measure service effectiveness in meeting that specific goal or objective.

Efficiency can be measured in terms of the effect of service processes on the number of questions answered. In some cases, a greater question-answer rate may be possible with the use of better processes. For instance, different technology used for question distribution may increase the number of questions sent to information specialists per day and thus may increase the number of questions answered; or more appropriate training may prepare information specialists to answer more questions at a quicker pace. If current processes cause a number of questions to go unanswered, users may turn elsewhere for service. In this scenario, unanswered questions become a cost to the service; better processes (in terms of training, technology, etc.) could allow more questions to be answered, thus increasing efficiency.

Measuring and Analyzing Web Site Visitors

Besides measuring question-answer rate, it is sometimes helpful to measure numbers of incoming questions and numbers of users visiting the AskA service site to view supporting resources (e.g., FAQs, archive, etc.) and submit questions. Many Web site owners use the "hit" method to collect statistics on how many users visit a site. This technique of data collection consists of measuring the number of times a particular document or image is transmitted, or downloaded, by the Internet Service Provider (ISP) to the user's client software. While many services use this method to measure numbers of site visitors, it is relatively unreliable in that it does not account for multiple file transfers during the loading of one Web page during a single user's visit.

User demographics can also be automatically determined to a degree. Auditing programs can measure the number of hits from distinct IP addresses. Web site owners typically distinguish users by their servers' domain extension (e.g., .com, .edu, .gov, etc.). Using this method, it is also possible to determine the countries users are connecting from. Measuring user demographics in this way does not provide the most accurate or complete information, but can provide some insight into the types of accounts to which users have access (e.g., university server, K–12 school server from a given U.S. state, commercial Internet provider).

When measuring numbers of visitors, or "hits," users should beware that they are not placing too much emphasis on the popularity of the site. Instead this information should be used to record statistics for service planning. For instance, services can identify peak question times during the year (especially appropriate for K–12 services that normally have highest numbers during in-school periods) in order to anticipate staff and other resource needs for a given time. Or they can identify the Web pages, or locations of pages, that are most often visited in order to decide where to place important information about the service.

Performance Assessment

Particular attention should be paid to the job performance of information specialists as it is their responses that become the main product of the service. Standards and criteria for job performance are outlined in training objectives for each individual service (see Module 3: Training). Results of performance evaluations can lead to revision of training programs and materials for new staff or development of new job improvement solutions (e.g., job aids, refresher training course, etc.) for current staff.

Impact on Users

Since many AskA services include some type of user education as a goal or objective of service, it only makes sense to assess the change in knowledge, skill, or attitude on the part of the user as a result of using the service. However, this is extremely difficult to measure since many users may use the service only once (not always providing adequate opportunity for effective learning), and the possible effects caused by a digital reference transaction are often affected by many other factors—user's previous knowledge, knowledge gained from participation in other educational activities, etc. Aside from the conceptual difficulties, the actual testing process creates many challenges as well.

While this Starter Kit cannot provide solutions or examples for digital reference impact studies, it presents this type of study as a possible area of evaluation. Perhaps AskA services can work with educators to guide students in interactions with the service and measure some aspect of learning as a result of the interaction (e.g., change in knowledge, skill, or attitude). For instance, a library-based service could measure users' development of research skills as a result of the service. This may work better for services that incorporate a fairly large instructional component (e.g., provide guidance in problem-solving skills, encourage motivation in subject areas) into their responses than those who simply provide factual answers or references.

6.2 How to Evaluate

This section discusses standards and methods for evaluating digital reference services.

Standards for Digital Reference Evaluation

As previously mentioned, evaluation of AskA services should measure how well the service meets its identified goals and objectives. However, service goals and objectives don't always provide quantitative standards by which to judge specific aspects of service (e.g., user satisfaction, efficiency of software work-flow package, information specialist performance and response quality). Standards for traditional reference services are mostly very general, leaving individual libraries to set their own standards for quality or compare their situations to those of other libraries (Allen, 1995).

Digital reference services can look to the Virtual Reference Desk's "Facets of Quality for K–12 Digital Reference Services" (see Module 1: Informing) to identify evaluation questions and possible factors. Although the 12 identified "facets" are not based on quantitative measurements, they provide a set of characteristics and features that indicate quality of the question-answer process as well as overall service development and management. Table 6-2 reviews the facets of quality in the context of a digital reference service evaluation.

Table 6-2: Facets of Quality and Possible Evaluation Questions and Factors

Facet of Quality	Sample Questions for Evaluation	Related Service Factors
User Transaction		
1. Accessible	• To what extent can all interested users access the service through channels provided (e.g., e-mail address, Web form)? • To what extent can all interested users easily navigate service Web resources?	• User technical capabilities • User special needs • User satisfaction with Internet resources
2. Prompt turnaround	Are questions answered within a timeframe that is useful for the user?	• User awareness of service limitations • User satisfaction with turnaround time • IS performance (i.e., training must prepare IS to respond within required time limit) • Effectiveness of systems and procedures for question-answer flow
3. Sets user expectations	Are users informed as to important service policies and qualifications such as: • Time frame for returning response? • Format of response (e.g., what it will include, where response will appear)? • Rate of questions answered by service? • Expert qualifications of service, those providing answers (information specialists), and resources consulted to find answers?	• User awareness of scope, limitations of service • IS performance (communicating relevant information in responses) • Extent to which supporting Internet resources contain relevant information regarding service

4. Interactive	• Does the service provide opportunities for users to communicate necessary information to information specialists and to clarify vague user questions?
	  ◊ Are mechanisms in place to capture important user information such as age or grade level, other information sources checked, contact information, etc.?
	  ◊ Are mechanisms in place to capture user feedback?
		• Ability to collect user information such as:
		  ◊ Characteristics and demographics
		  ◊ Technical capabilities
		  ◊ Information needs
		  ◊ Special needs
		• Ability to collect feedback on service in terms of
		  ◊ Satisfaction with response and q/a process
		  ◊ Satisfaction with service Internet resources
		  ◊ Benefits gained and activities performed as result of using service (follow-through)

Facet of Quality	Sample Questions for Evaluation	Related Service Factors
User Transaction		
5. Instructive	Do information specialists and supporting resources provide instruction in subject knowledge and information literacy?	• Helpfulness of specific response components • Ability of response to provide users with follow-through strategies
Service Development and Management		
6. Authoritative	Do information specialists have the necessary knowledge and educational background in the service's given subject area or skill in order to qualify as an expert?	• Ability of policy to establish required skills for information specialists • Extent of screening process for accepting information specialists • Availability of continued education or training in subject area
7. Trained information specialists	Does the service offer effective orientation or training processes to prepare information specialists to respond to inquiries using clear and effective language and following service response guidelines?	• IS performance on the job • Increase in skills as result of participation in training program and materials • User satisfaction with information specialists' response—content, tone, etc. (See Module 3.4 for additional information on evaluating training programs for digital reference.)
8. Private	Are all communications between users and information specialists held in complete privacy?	Ability of policy to define measures to restrict public access to private user information in Internet information resources and responses
9. Reviewed	How often does the service evaluate processes and services in terms of information specialists' responses, user satisfaction and information specialist satisfaction?	• Implementation of regular evaluation schedule • Nature of evaluation questions and methods • Data analysis and revision decisions
10. Unbiased	What measures are taken to restrict promotion of commercial products or personal or institutional opinions in order to protect quality, credibility, and efficiency of service?	• Ability of policy to restrict bias • Effectiveness of training program to prepare IS to avoid bias in responses (as measured by IS performance) • Lack of bias in supporting Internet resources

Facet of Quality	Sample Questions for Evaluation	Related Service Factors
Service Development and Managment		

11. Provides access to related information	In what capacities does the service offer access to supporting resources and information (e.g., archive, FAQs, references to related information sources)? (See Module 5, Contributing)	• User satisfaction with Internet information resources (type, format, content, usability)
		• Quality of resources
		  ◊ Readability
		  ◊ Ability to meet user needs as identified by incoming questions
		  ◊ Extent to which user privacy is maintained
		  ◊ Accessibility (e.g., adequate search engines, organization of information)

12. Publicized	To what extent does the service inform potential users of the value that can be gained from use of the service? (See Module 5, Contributing)	• User awareness of scope and limitations of service • Quantity of incoming user questions • Implementation of regular publicity plan

Methods for Digital Reference Evaluation

The following methods are borrowed from literature on traditional library reference evaluation and experiences of existing AskA services. They are presented as suggestions and examples.

"Unobtrusive" Evaluation

Unobtrusive reference service evaluation refers to studies where test subjects (usually reference librarians) are not aware of the test being conducted. Proxies acting as library patrons approach the reference desk with questions (to which answers are previously known) in order to test various aspects of reference service (e.g., response accuracy, question-negotiation skills).

Background

The library community has been involved in the research and practice of unobtrusive reference service evaluation for about 30 years. In 1968, Terence Crowley developed an unobtrusive evaluation technique that was later revised by Thomas Childers[25] (Allen,

---

[25] See Crowley, Terence and Childers (1971).

1995). Since then, many unobtrusive reference studies have been conducted[26] (over 20 of which identified a 55% correct response rate to factual reference questions [Allen, 1995]).

Advantages of unobtrusive studies in library reference according to Allen (1995) and Murfin and Gugelchuk (1987) include these:

- Since staff is unaware of assessment, they are able to respond as they would during a usual reference transaction.
- Results can be used to identify areas requiring staff training.
- Studies can be adapted for use in a single site (library).

Unobtrusive studies in library reference have been met with some criticism over the years. Among the arguments of those opposing such studies include (Allen, 1995; Murfin & Gugelchuk, 1987) these:

- The fact that test subjects are not informed raises ethical concerns.
- Questions are mainly factual and fail to represent wide range of typical user questions.
- Studies mainly concentrate on accuracy of response as the single factor in reference transaction.

Anticipated Uses of Unobtrusive Study in Digital Reference

Unobtrusive evaluation can be easily adapted to a digital reference context and for an individual AskA service. This type of study may even be better suited to unobtrusive evaluation than traditional reference. Instead of physically approaching a reference desk or making a phone call, the proxy can e-mail a query to a service (or group of services) in order to test several aspects of the service such as:

- Accuracy of response
- Tone and clarity of response
- Turnaround time
- Interactivity (e.g., query negotiation)
- Setting of expectations for users (e.g., nature of response, turnaround time, etc.).

In addition to participating in a digital reference transaction, a researcher can also review a sample of previously answered questions in a service's archive—another form of unobtrusive evaluation. Unlike most traditional reference transactions, many digital reference transactions are recorded and archived somewhere—whether or not the archive is made available to the public. While this less interactive type of analysis does not allow

---

[26] For an overview of unobtrusive evaluation in library reference services, see Crews (1988).

the researcher the experience of an actual question-answer transaction, it still provides adequate information regarding the nature of the response including all communications that ensued (assuming all pieces of the transaction are kept intact in one message or related string of messages).

In fact, service administrators may use this method on a regular basis or during training to assess the performance of information specialists. If an information specialist's main job task is to write responses, this sort of assessment can provide valid data on his or her performance.

Although the authors are currently unaware of any formal external unobtrusive digital reference studies, they are aware that some agencies and individuals have tested various services for the purposes of their own research and publication. For instance, journalists have submitted fictional questions to services in order to gather information for reviews of educational Internet resources.[27] However, like reference librarians who are often surprised and disappointed upon finding that researchers have tested them "behind their backs," AskA service administrators also feel slighted when reviewers use results of a limited number of question-answer transactions to represent the quality of overall service to a public audience.

User Survey Method

While unobtrusive evaluation methods can measure many things regarding quality of information specialists' responses and the response process, they lack the ability to accurately assess user satisfaction with the service or information specialist satisfaction with various aspects of the service (e.g., training, question-answer process, etc.). The method of employing user surveys allows services to gather affective data and suggestions on specific reference components from large groups of stakeholders and audiences.

In traditional library reference evaluation, user surveys have been distributed to gather feedback on satisfaction with the result of the reference transaction, the reference service provided, and the attitude, abilities, and other characteristics of reference staff. Limitations of such evaluation methods include the presence of response bias, or the inclination of users to react as they think they are expected to. Because of the possibility of response bias and the fact that survey instruments are so difficult and time consuming

---

[27] Hays (1997) and "Ask A Librarian…" (1998) test the KidsConnect question-answer service in an unobtrusive manner.

to create, it has been suggested that libraries use standard instruments[28] instead of designing their own (Allen, 1995). Currently, there are no standard survey instruments for evaluating AskA services, but this section can provide suggestions and examples for creating original instruments.

Designing Questionnaires for Reference Evaluation

Morgan (1995, pp.142–147) offers the following recommendations for creating surveys to evaluate reference service performance assessment:

- Keep it short
- Include all relevant questions
- Include adequate white space between questions
- Include questions of interest to respondents to encourage further participation
- Keep instructions consistent (e.g., use one type of "check" method for closed questions, such as circling, check mark, etc.)
- Use simple language, free of jargon and acronyms
- State questions clearly in order to communicate their exact meaning (e.g., avoid double negatives, ambiguous wording, etc.).

Survey Use in Digital Reference

Distributing and analyzing surveys from users of digital reference services is relatively easy and has been useful in helping AskA services identify areas for revision. Advantages in conducting digital reference user surveys include these:

- Surveys can be distributed directly to e-mail accounts of users who have previously asked questions of the service, making the survey directly accessible.
- Surveys can also be created as Web forms, also making the survey easily accessible and allowing the creation of scripts to automatically tabulate responses. (Note: Services should restrict access to a Web-based survey in order to filter out those who have not previously participated in a question-answer transaction.)
- Users can return surveys simply by replying to an e-mail message or automatically submitting it from a Web form, possibly increasing the return rate over paper surveys that have to be mailed or physically delivered.
- Surveys can be sent to users in such a manner that a previous question-answer interaction is included in the message—this can help refresh users' memories

---

[28] One standard survey form for library reference assessment is the Wisconsin-Ohio form. See Bunge (1985) and Murfin and Gugelchuk (1987).

regarding their use of the service and help the service analyze user responses in the context of users' actual experiences.

- Content of surveys can focus on several specific aspects of service (e.g., components of message, information specialists' tone, turnaround time, etc.) as well as user demographic and technical information. This provides services with a targeted overview of user satisfaction and user requirements of service.

Common issues targeted in surveys for digital reference include these:

- User information

    ◊ User demographics (e.g., grade, profession) including capacity in which question was asked (e.g., a library media specialist may ask a question for professional development or may send a question on behalf of a third-grade student)
    ◊ User technical capabilities (e.g., ability to contact service, access response, etc.)
    ◊ Ability to use information or to access resources referenced in response
    ◊ Number of times user has submitted questions to the service (for identification of repeat users).

- Satisfaction with response content and process

    ◊ Extent to which response answered user question (e.g., relevance or effectiveness of information provided)
    ◊ Satisfaction with amount of information included in the message
    ◊ Helpfulness of standard response components (e.g., resources referred, inclusion of user question, etc.)
    ◊ Readability and comprehensibility of response
    ◊ Satisfaction with turnaround time of response
    ◊ Consistency of response in terms of user expectations.

- Follow-through

    ◊ Capacity in which response will be used (e.g., school assignment, personal interest, lesson planning).

- Publicity

    ◊ Information source that originally informed user of service (e.g., Web site, brochure, conference presentation, etc.)
    ◊ Other individuals with whom user communicated regarding question creation or response contents (e.g., teacher, colleagues, etc.).

- General feedback

    ◊ Willingness to use service again
    ◊ Benefits gained by user as a result of service (e.g., save time, money, etc.)
    ◊ Open suggestions, comments, etc.

Some services may also choose to include questions relating to accessibility and usefulness of Internet resources such as archive, FAQs, links to related sites, etc. However, some services wish to focus questions on the question-answer process separately from related resources.

An example of a questionnaire used to evaluate an AskA service is found in Figure 6-1: AskERIC Q & A Survey.

Besides questionnaires, other survey activities include discussion groups and interviews. These methods can be used to capture the same type of information as a questionnaire, but they add an interactive element. During these interactive sessions, questions and responses can be clarified, respondents can communicate nonverbal reactions, and conversation can lead to more in-depth issues (Morgan, 1995). In a traditional library situation, discussion groups and interviews are usually face-to-face meetings of one or more users and facilitators or interviewers. In digital reference settings, the conversations can occur virtually. For instance, a service can set up an expert panel of representative users to launch discussions about responses, Web resources, processes, and other issues identified for evaluation. This should be done with a controlled group of users who express interest in participating in such a survey.

Figure 6-1 shows a portion of the AskERIC Q&A Survey conducted in 1998.

Figure 6-1 AskERIC Q&A Survey

AskERIC Q&A Survey

Thank you for recently using the AskERIC Question Answering Service. In order to help us better serve our patrons we are conducting a brief survey. Please take a few minutes to answer the following questions. Your help would be greatly appreciated.

AskERIC respects the privacy of its users. Participation in the survey is voluntary, and all information will be kept anonymous and confidential. Your name will not be used in any way, and no one will know about your specific answers except the study researchers.

Thank you for your time and cooperation.

The AskERIC Staff

1. How did you send a message to AskERIC?
      A. e-mail
      B. Web form

2. What is your profession?
      A. librarian
      B. K-12 teacher
      C. pre-K teacher/caregiver
      D. administrator
      E. student
      F. faculty
      G. parent
      H. government official
      I. other_____

3. In what capacity did you request information from AskERIC?
      A. librarian
      B. K-12 teacher
      C. pre-K teacher/caregiver
      D. administrator
      E. student
      F. faculty
      G. parent
      H. government official
      I. other_____

4. Have you used AskERIC more than once?
        A. yes
        B. no

        4.1 If yes, how many times have you used the service in the past year?
            A. 1-3
            B. 4-6
            C. 7-10
            D. more than 10

5. Was the information provided relevant to your question?
        A. yes
        B. no

6. Did the information provided lead you to an answer to your question?
        A. yes
        B. no

7. How are you using the information gained from the service?
        A. research
        B. classroom implementation
        C. personal
        D. career preparation
        E. other_____

8. Has the service saved you time?
        A. yes
        B. no

        8.1 money?
            A. yes
            B. no

9. Please rate the helpfulness of the different components of an AskERIC response. (1=LEAST HELPFUL, 5 = MOST HELPFUL, NA =NOT APPLICABLE). Please note that not all components are present in every response.

ERIC citations	1	2	3	4	5	NA
Internet sites	1	2	3	4	5	NA
Listservs	1	2	3	4	5	NA
Organizations	1	2	3	4	5	NA
Other Resources	1	2	3	4	5	NA

10. Was the information easy to read?
        A. yes
        B. no

        10.1. Why/Why not?

Other Methods for Measuring Staff Performance

Aside from unobtrusive testing and user survey distribution, there are other possible methods for directly evaluating information specialists' performance in creating digital reference responses. (Also see Module 3: Training, for more suggestions on evaluating IS performance during and after training). Possible methods include the following (services can combine the methods if desired):

- **Peer assessment**—AskA services can establish systems whereby senior information specialists (those who have demonstrated quality performance) assess the responses of newer information specialists and provide feedback on their performance. Some services implement this method by splitting their information specialist (expert) base into distinct groups (based on expertise area or some other grouping). Leaders or moderators of each group regularly assess group members' responses according to a set of criteria (e.g., inclusion of required response components, friendly tone, etc.) and then provide each information specialist with feedback to help them improve future responses.

- **Grading or Tracking**—Grading or tracking schemes can be implemented in order to assign values to information specialists' responses. This method allows services to judge individual information specialists in a consistent manner. Information specialists can be assessed over time to track improvement and make decisions regarding advancement or discontinuation with service. (For an example of a grading scheme for AskA service responses, see "The MadSci Moderators' Manual" *http://www.madsci.org/ask_expert/moderators.html*)

- **Self-assessment**—Some services may choose to implement a program where information specialists evaluate their own performance according to predefined standards. Some form of recording should be in place to help information specialists track their performance and report results to service administrators. Recording can be facilitated with instruments such as checklists to be filled out after each response.

Regardless of the methods used for performance evaluation, it is important to inform information specialists (or other staff) of their level of performance and suggest ways for them to improve. (For suggestions on providing feedback, see Module 3.4). Common issues derived from performance evaluations (e.g., all information specialists fail to include a required response component) indicate that there may be a need to revise training programs or reinforcement resources and activities for current staff.

6.3 The AskA Service Evaluation Process

Evaluation of AskA services should be included as part of the overall service plan and to be most effective should occur on an ongoing basis. Currently, most services do not conduct ongoing formal evaluation activities because of constraints on capacity and time; it is suggested that services start slowly by focusing on one or two areas and then build on once comfortable methods and strategies are in place. Of course those services that have pressure from funding organizations do not always have the luxury of choosing evaluation areas and schedules. In any case, it is important for services to always keep an eye out for potential evaluation areas (see Tables 6-1 and 6-2 for sample areas) so that they can be properly examined at the appropriate time.

Planning Issues

Once a service has identified target issues and questions for evaluation, it needs to plan the evaluation in order to ensure that the goals are achieved. There are many issues to consider when planning an evaluation in any context.[29] The steps below are described in the context of digital reference evaluation:

1. **Creation of evaluation goals.** There should be a defined purpose for conducting the evaluation (aside from the charge by a sponsoring organization). The goal should reflect larger service goals and objectives and should indicate the target evaluation areas. Below are examples of evaluation goals for AskA services:

- Measure user satisfaction regarding standard components and language used in responses.
- Assess performance of information specialists in completing the response process according to service policies and procedures.
- Evaluate the usefulness of work-flow software in terms of routing questions to information specialists, assisting information specialists during the response process, and archiving question-answer sets.

2. **Formation of evaluation team.** The team approach to planning and implementing evaluation of digital reference services is beneficial to the overall effort. As is true of traditional reference service evaluation, digital reference evaluation efforts are frequently too large for one staff member to accomplish individually, and it is helpful to gain perspectives of different people both internal and external to the service. By inviting

---

[29] This section is adapted from Smith and Costello (1989). See Hernon and McClure (1987) for discussion of steps involved in establishing formal evaluation systems for reference services (pp. 112–128).

input from service staff—especially those whose work is being evaluated—a sense of trust of the evaluation effort can be established. When forming the evaluation team, services may consider outside researchers who can provide an objective approach. This can include a supporting organization's evaluation department, graduate students at a sponsoring university, etc.

3. Identify major questions and sub-questions. Besides establishing goals to guide the evaluation, services should identify general and specific questions that they expect the evaluation to answer. For instance, services may wish to know if users are generally satisfied with responses to their questions. More specifically, a service may want to examine to what extent users are satisfied with specific components of their responses, such as the list of references included, instructions for accessing resources, and the brief factual answer.

4. Select procedures or methods to collect information. For each question and sub-question identified, services should establish a plan for collecting information to address it. For instance, in order to find out if information specialists are using clear language in their responses, the evaluation team may propose to review a sample of archived responses.

5. Establish data collection schedule. It helps to establish a time period in which evaluation activities will take place. This assists the service in completing activities in a realistic and useful timeframe so that results can be used to make necessary decisions. It also helps to balance multiple activities that are sometimes required of evaluation efforts.

6. Identify types and sample of respondents. If planned procedures require the participation of individuals to provide information (e.g., questionnaires, etc.), the evaluation team should identify who and how many should be asked to provide information. For instance, should a user satisfaction questionnaire be distributed to all users who submit questions and receive responses in a given period of time? Should it be distributed to only a sample of users who receive responses (e.g., every third user)? How should users be chosen to participate in an expert panel discussion group?

7. Create plan for analyzing and interpreting information. Once information is received through the methods pursued, it must be analyzed and interpreted in such a way that evaluation questions can be effectively answered. Information received should be compared against evaluative criteria. For instance, the criteria for efficiency of work-flow software could include that 90% of incoming questions must be routed to information specialists on the day they are received, 100% of information specialists' responses must be automatically saved in the archive, etc.

8. Create evaluation management plan. Besides planning a basic schedule of activities, larger evaluative efforts may require plans that outline the budget and personnel needed to conduct the evaluation.

9. Outline reporting methods. Depending on the purpose and goals and evaluation, reporting methods can include brief internal reports for the service staff reference or formal research reports for a sponsoring organization. Regardless of the specific format, evaluation reports should be written clearly, in the context of the intended evaluation audience, and should encourage some type of action in response to the evaluation results (Hernon & McClure, 1987). It is helpful to establish a plan for reporting before the actual evaluation occurs in order to ensure that reporting activities are conducted appropriately and in a timely manner.

Using Results

Once the evaluation has been conducted and information has been analyzed and reported, results can be used to improve service. Evaluation results do not always provide clear-cut solutions for problems identified but can be helpful in starting initial discussion regarding ways to improve the service. This discussion should involve staff affected, and priorities should be set for developing and implementing solutions.

Examples of solutions based on evaluation results are presented below:

- Evaluation indicates that users have difficulty understanding some of the content that is regularly included in responses (e.g., codes referring to service resources). This could lead to several solutions: eliminating codes, providing definitions for codes, spelling out codes, etc. The service may decide to test various solutions and then survey users again to see which are most helpful.

- Evaluation finds that many information specialists refer users to Web sites that are of poor quality and are inappropriate for the user audience (e.g., K–12 students). Solutions may include a new component of staff training introducing information specialists to criteria for assessing Web sites suitable for inclusion in responses. In addition, such criteria can be included in a job aid for current information specialists.

- Evaluation of user questions finds that 45% of incoming queries are out of scope for the service. Solutions can include revising the service Web pages and promotional materials to more accurately reflect service scope (e.g., including examples of appropriate questions) or instituting user education programs (e.g., presentations to educators, students, and parents) to communicate important information regarding the service and appropriate use.

Module 6 Summary

This section provided suggestions and examples for possible areas and methods of AskA service evaluation.

- Evaluation of digital reference service is a new area that can learn from research in evaluation of traditional library reference service.

- The primary reason for conducting formal evaluation of AskA services is to ensure that goals of the service and organization are being met most efficiently and effectively. Evaluations of digital reference services can be both formative (for improvement purposes) and summative (for decision making) in nature.

- In deciding what to evaluate, services should examine current detectors, rules, and effectors. Sample areas include quantity of questions and users; staff performance; and service impact on users.

- Standards for digital reference evaluation are based on the Virtual Reference Desk's "Facets of Quality for K–12 Digital Reference Services."

- Methods for digital reference evaluation can include unobtrusive evaluation and user survey. Additional methods are used specifically for staff performance assessment: peer assessment, grading or tracking, and self-assessment.

- The AskA service evaluation process consists of an extensive but important planning phase including the creation of goals, formation of evaluation team, identification of questions, selection of methods, creation of data collection schedule, identification of respondents, and creation of plans for analysis and interpretation of information, management of evaluation, and reporting of results.

- Evaluation results can be used to start discussion of identified problems and possible solutions.

Work Sheet 6-1: AskA Service Evaluation Planning Table[30]

This work sheet is designed to help you organize information while planning an evaluation of an AskA service. While this table may not allow extensive note-taking in each specific area, it can facilitate the initial brainstorming process.

Primary Question	Sub-questions	Collection Procedures/ Methods	Evaluation Criteria	Respondents	Sample	Collection Schedule (dates)	Budget	Personnel

[30] Adapted from Smith & Costello (1989).

Conclusion

Module Profile

This module provides a conclusion to the *AskA Starter Kit*. At the end of this module, you will be able to achieve the following goal:

Goal Place the Starter Kit into a larger framework that incorporates an action-based agenda and a vision for the future of digital reference.

Prerequisites Before reading this conclusion, an organization should have completed the six modules representing the steps involved in building and maintaining a digital reference service:

1. Collect information on the general digital reference field and existing AskA services (Module 1: Informing).
2. Determine the best way to build and maintain digital reference service within the organization (Module 2: Planning).
3. Plan, produce, implement, and manage training programs for service staff and information specialists (Module 3: Training).
4. Create a prototype and conduct a pilot test of an AskA service (Module 4: Prototyping).
5. Manage service development and operations and build partnerships to gain necessary support and share processes (see Module 5: Contributing).
6. Plan and implement evaluation of an AskA service and use results to improve service (Module 6: Evaluating).

Objectives At the completion of this module, you will be able to achieve the following objectives:

1. Understand the importance of the human intermediary in digital reference service (providing contextual information in response to user needs).
2. Understand the role of technology in connecting users with information.
3. State the main challenges for digital reference service in the future.
4. Apply suggestions and examples from this Starter Kit to the development of a new AskA service.

Summary and Challenges for the Future

The implicit promise of the information age is context. Those seeking information are not looking for Web pages, books, or articles; rather, they are looking for answers—solutions to a problem grounded in their situation. What is a pearl of wisdom one day can be a useless piece of trivia on another. Discerning user needs and creating context are inherently human activities, because they involve the process of communication—not the mechanical processes of archiving and delivery. Therefore the needed intermediary of the information age is not a Web page but rather a human being.

The goal of any technology is to become invisible. Technology is a means to an end. If we are to fulfill the promise of the information age and connect those with problems with those with answers, we must make the technology that we use transparent. E-mail clients, Web sites, and modems must appear to vanish as users connect to experts. The paradox here is that only by improving technology, and the processes that utilize these technologies, can we make the tools, products, etc. disappear.

The great challenge before digital reference services (from those who research them to those who use them to those who provide them) is to achieve a seamless integration of resources, people, and technology. This may well be Plato's unattainable ideal, but it is a goal to strive for. Certainly digital reference is in its infancy and has much to learn as it grows. Challenges remain ahead:

- **How do we incorporate real-time communications into our services?** There is little doubt this Starter Kit assumes a heavy amount of e-mail and asynchronous service. How can we build models with real-time chats and video conferencing?

- **How do we build an economy of reference?** This is more than determining a "per question" price. It relates to how we value experts, manage and allocate resources, create barter arrangements, constrain transactions, build policy for the fair use of services, and, yes, cost services.

- **What standardization is needed?** What are the technical and policy standards that we need to put in place to create seamless navigation from reference service to reference service, and reference service to resource?

- **Is fragmentation of digital reference inevitable?** Does digital reference need to be different for libraries, education, and business? This Starter Kit was written on the assumption that the challenges facing all of these sectors are common and can best be explored and solved together.

In spite of these and many other questions, the outlook for digital reference services is bright. As large organizations move to the Web to conduct their day-to-day operations, traditional areas of customer service, commerce, and quality management will be challenged to adapt to the Internet environment. With the entry of large private and public institutions into the realms of digital reference (be they called help desks, customer service, reference, or AskA) comes increased investment, understanding, and tools. The question for the readers of this document is: Do you want to be the early explorers of these domains, or wait for the problems to be solved? If you wait, are you confident that corporations, government, or other sectors will consider your needs and views as they deploy their systems?

By working through this Starter Kit you now have the tools to create AskA services. Hopefully you have a picture of the needs of your organization. Potentially you are returning to this text with a service established. What you must realize is that even though the ink is dry and the cover bound, this book is still being written. Your experience, your trials, and your resources will shape its evolution.

Where to Go From Here

So, where to go from here? The best answer is simply to start. Start learning more by visiting the services discussed in this kit. Start planning by surveying the needs of your organization. Start training in order to get your experts online and ready. Start prototyping by downloading sample software or even an e-mail client. Start contributing to the community through your service—tell us what you're doing, share your expertise. Start evaluating by asking the hardest questions of all for those who have an AskA service—is it being done well, and does it make a difference?

Stuart Sutton, a professor at Syracuse University's School of Information Studies, once said, "The future does not come shrink-wrapped." Projects such as the Virtual Reference Desk and Ask Dr. Math and companies such as Remedy Corporation are creating software for AskA services, but they have just begun. The initial phase of software development will be sample code, test bed projects, and source code that can be adapted. Efforts are underway to create standards for the interchange of questions and reference interviews. All of these efforts are in their infancies. Even the long established help desk software requires extensive customization (and considerable cost) to create a workable system.

Now is the time to get involved. Now is the time to put your voice and the needs of your users into a larger dialogue about how to conduct digital reference. If you're a library, lend your knowledge of the reference process. If you're a business, share your understanding of customer service. If you're an educational institution, share your experiences in pedagogy and curriculum. We stand at the dawn of a communications revolution, a revolution that will place context above data, and people above Web pages. You are invited to be a part of this new era.

Module Summary

This section provided a summary of the Starter Kit and a framework for digital reference now and in the future.

- Human intermediaries are crucial in digital reference service in order to determine user needs and communicate information in context.

- Technology for digital reference must be improved in order to appear seamless to the user.

- The greatest challenge for digital reference services is to achieve seamless integration of resources, people, and technology. Other challenges include incorporation of real-time communications, creation of a reference economy, development of standards for technology and policies of digital reference, and exploration of common issues across various digital reference contexts.

- Organizations interested in building AskA services can begin immediately using the suggestions and examples from the six modules of the "Starter Kit." Suggested activities include visiting existing AskA services, surveying needs of organization, developing a training program and training experts, downloading sample software, sharing expertise with the digital reference community, and planning for service evaluation.

About The Virtual Reference Desk

The Virtual Reference Desk (VRD) is creating the foundations for a national cooperative digital reference service. The project is sponsored by the National Library of Education (NLE) and the ERIC Clearinghouse on Information & Technology, with support from the Office of Science and Technology Policy. The Virtual Reference Desk seeks to identify and provide the resources necessary to link all K-12 community members (e.g., students, educators, parents, etc.) to necessary expertise in order to satisfy information needs.

The goals of the project include research into current ways in which K-12 community members receive answers to questions on the Internet and development of a national collaborative network of Internet-based question-answering services.

What is Digital Reference?. . .

Digital reference services, also called "Ask-An-Expert" (or "AskA") services, are Internet-based question and answer services that connect users with individuals who possess specialized subject or skill expertise. As opposed to static Web pages, digital reference services use the Internet to place *people* in contact with *people* who can answer specific questions and instruct users on developing certain skills.

Resources and Services Include. . .

- **Database of question/answer services**—The **AskA+ Locator** contains a collection of over 70 quality AskA services for the K-12 community. Services can be searched or browsed (*http://www.vrd.org/locator/index.html*).

- **Virtual Reference Desk Web site (*www.vrd.org*)**—This central access point for digital reference provides information on exemplary AskA services and offers resources to help organizations build and maintain new AskA services, including training materials and quality criteria.

- **Starter Kit**—This instructional resource guides organizations in the development of new AskA services in their areas of expertise by providing "how-to" advice and methods based on experiences of exemplary services and in-depth research.

- **Dig_Ref Listserv**—A discussion group open to those interested in all contexts of digital reference service. Current subscribers include those working in libraries, education, business, government and other sectors, both nationally and internationally.

> For more information on
> the Virtual Reference Desk, contact
> ***vrd@vrd.org*** or **(800) 464-9107**.

Glossary

The following terms are defined in the context of digital reference service as outlined in this *Starter Kit.*

Archive: A stored collection of question-and-answer sets. May be publicly accessible online or retained for a service's private use.

AskA Consortium: A group of AskA services in a cooperative network that seeks to provide resources (computing infrastructure, funding, and knowledge) to its members and guides the overall Virtual Reference Desk project.

AskA+ Locator: Searchable database of over 70 AskA services that serve the K–12 community and meet some minimal quality criteria as identified by an expert panel. Detailed descriptions are available for each service in the Locator for assistance in selecting the most appropriate service for a given situation.
http://www.vrd.org/locator/index.html

AskA services: Internet-based question-and-answer services that connect users with individuals who possess specialized subject or skill expertise. Also known as digital reference services, provide human expertise through question-answer services on the Internet. So called for services such as Ask-A-Scientist or Ask-A-Volcanologist, these services take questions through e-mail and the World Wide Web.

Blueprint: Graphical representation of the conceptual framework and methodology of an AskA service.

Contributing: The ongoing process by which an AskA service offers information services to the user community (e.g., frequently K–12 educators, students, and parents) and shares expertise and experience with its supporting organization and digital reference community.

Detectors: Mechanism for acquiring information about an organization's environment. Information gained is used to ensure that an AskA service meets stakeholder and user needs and uses the most efficient means to accomplish goals.

Digital reference: Field of information science focusing on the creation and operation of Internet information systems to satisfy user needs. Although many concepts and processes have roots in traditional library reference, digital reference applies to Internet-based question and answer services in many contexts including education and business.

Digital reference services: Internet-based question-answer and referral services that reach a wide audience on a wide range of topics. Services can be operated by libraries, professional associations, educational institutions, and other types of organizations that can connect users with individuals possessing specialized subject or skill expertise. Also referred to as AskA services.

Effectors: Sets of services offered to users or others on the Internet in order to meet reference needs.

ERIC (Educational Resources Information Center): National education information system sponsored by the Office of Educational Research and Improvement in the U. S. Department of Education and the National Library of Education. Established in 1966, ERIC produces the largest database of education information in the world.

Evaluation: Systematic process by which the value and efficiency of a product or process is determined according to set criteria.

Expert panel: Group of representatives from AskA services and other related organizations who identified the quality criteria for K–12 digital reference services and selected seven exemplary services that fit the criteria. *http://www.vrd.org/panel/members.html*

Experts: Staff or volunteers possessing special skills and knowledge derived from training, education, and experience. Also referred to as information specialists when providing expert information to digital reference service users.

Extensiveness: Percentage of incoming questions answered.

FAQ (Frequently Asked Questions): Document containing commonly asked questions and their answers. Often provided as part of a digital reference service's Web site.

Formative evaluation: Method of evaluation that focuses on issues of improvement. (Example: How can services more effectively meet user needs?)

GEM (Gateway to Educational Materials): A metadata project developing vocabularies and standards to allow educators to find lesson plans and other educational materials quickly and easily on the Internet. GEM is sponsored by the U.S. Department of Education's National Library of Education and is a special project of the ERIC Clearinghouse on Information & Technology at Syracuse University. *http://www.thegateway.org*

Goals: Positioning statements defining what an AskA service expects to achieve.

Grading or tracking: Evaluative method where alphanumeric values are assigned to information specialists' responses in order to rate performance.

Holland's Performance System: A means to describe any organization by detectors (the means the organization has to gain information about the world), rules (the processes an organization uses to determine a course of action based on information from detectors) and effectors (mechanisms an organization has in place to affect the environment or its place in that environment). This scheme of detectors-rules-effectors was developed by John Holland of the University of Michigan.

Information specialists: Human intermediaries that direct a course of action for questions received by AskA services. May also be subject experts to whom questions are submitted.

Instructional design: The systematic process of planning events to facilitate learning. Can be applied to planning of training programs and materials for digital reference service staff.

Internet Engineering Task Force: "The Internet Engineering Task Force (IETF) is a large open international community of network designers, operators, vendors, and researchers concerned with the evolution of the Internet architecture and the smooth operation of the Internet. It is open to any interested individual." *http://www.ietf.org/overview.html*

Internet Public Library (IPL): A project of the University of Michigan School of Information that provides Internet users with access to resources as well as digital reference service. *http://www.ipl.org*

Job aid: Supplemental resource intended to help the trainee come up to speed during training and to provide support for performance on the job.

Knowledge base: A distributed index of question-and-answer archives across all AskA services in the AskA Consortium. A planned resource of the Virtual Reference Desk Project.

Key detectors: Most important detectors in forming and maintaining decisions.

Metadata: Information about data itself. Metadata is used to understand, manage, and facilitate the sharing of and searching for materials on the World Wide Web.

Meta-description: Information about the core work-flow processes and functions in digital reference service.

Meta-triage: Function that is the backbone infrastructure that connects AskA services and end users together. It acts as the central switchboard for questions and answers traversing the Virtual Reference Desk's network of users and knowledge resources.

NLE (National Library of Education): Largest federally funded U.S. library that is entirely devoted to education. *http://www.ed.gov*

Objectives: Detailed statements describing how an AskA service intends to accomplish its mission. Also refers to key skills and knowledge AskA service staff is expected to achieve upon completion of training program.

Peer assessment: The assessment of AskA service staff performance by more experienced staff members according to specific criteria and with the goal of providing constructive feedback.

Pilot test: Preliminary process or "trial run" conducted as a basis for evaluation in order to improve services. Can be conducted to evaluate overall service or components of service such as training program.

Prototyping: The development of an initial functional, though incomplete, type or design of a product to be refined in successive tests. Digital reference services often engage in a prototyping phase in order to test service in a controlled environment before it is offered on a large scale.

Rules: Rules represent the actions of an AskA service based on the information from detectors. Rules may include such activities as question routing and archiving.

Self-assessment: Method of evaluation where information specialists rate their own performance according to a set of predetermined standards.

Service roles: Personnel positions found in AskA service organizations. Roles may include administrators, experts, information specialists, team leaders, and moderators.

Shrink-wrapped software: Fully functional and easily installed software to help automate AskA service processes.

Stakeholders: Outside agencies that have a guiding interest in a digital reference service.

Summative evaluation: Method of evaluation that focuses on the measurement of quality often for ultimate decision making purposes. (Example: To what extent is the AskA service achieving its goals?)

TCP/IP (Transmission Control Protocol/Internetworking Protocol): Software rules for allowing disparate networks to communicate.

Tracking: Process of capturing transaction information as questions are routed through an AskA service.

Triage: The sorting and allocation of questions in AskA services according to a system of priorities designed to maximize efficient response.

Unobtrusive evaluation: Method of evaluating a service where the test subjects are unaware of the test taking place.

Virtual Reference Desk (VRD): A project that is creating a national cooperative digital reference service in order to link the K-12 community with expertise to satisfy information needs. VRD seeks to identify and provide resources to organizations and individuals involved in providing knowledge and expertise to the K-12 community. *http://www.vrd.org*

AskA Service Directory

This directory includes AskA services highlighted in this Starter Kit. Additional AskA services serving K-12 students, educators, and others are available at the VRD AskA+ Locator *http://www.vrd.org/locator*

Ask Dr. Math
http://forum.swarthmore.edu/dr.math/
dr.math@forum.swarthmore.edu

Ask Dr. Math is a question-and-answer service for K–12 math teachers and students. The service provides an archive that is searchable by grade level and topic and includes such features as Frequently Asked Questions (FAQ), archives, and other resources. Ask Dr. Math is funded by the National Science Foundation and operates under the auspices of the Math Forum at Swarthmore College.

AskERIC
http://www.askeric.org
askeric@askeric.org

AskERIC is a personalized Internet-based AskA service providing education information to teachers, librarians, counselors, administrators, parents, and others throughout the United States and the world. It began in 1992 as a project of the ERIC Clearinghouse on Information & Technology at Syracuse University. Today, it encompasses the resources of the entire ERIC system and beyond. (See ERIC in the Glossary.)

Ask A NASA Scientist
http://imagine.gsfc.nasa.gov/docs/ask_astro/ask_an_astronomer.html
ask_astro@heasarc.gsfc.nasa.gov

Ask a NASA Scientist (formerly Ask a High Energy Astronomer) is a question and answer service for those interested in X-ray and gamma-ray astronomy. The service answers 100% of all questions received in 2-3 days. The site also includes an archive of previously-answered questions and teacher resources including study guides and lesson plans.

Ask A Volcanologist
http://volcano.und.nodak.edu/vwdocs/ask_a.html
[no e-mail submissions]

Ask a Volcanologist is a question-answering and referral service staffed by three professional volcanologists. The service attempts to answer all questions received within 3 days. Part of the larger VolcanoWorld Web site, a keyword-searchable FAQ of commonly asked questions on volcanoes, lesson plans for teachers, lessons and activities for students, and links to sources of other information about volcanoes are also available.

Ask Shamu

http://www.seaworld.org/ask_shamu/asindex.html
shamu@seaworld.org

Ask Shamu is a question and answer service for questions about the ocean and marine animals. Ask Shamu answers 100% of all questions received, and answers are short and factual with minimal references. An 800-number (1-800-23SHAMU) is provided for students to submit questions by telephone, and for teachers to request curriculum materials. The site also features a FAQ, curriculum guides, and more.

Ask the Optometrist

http://www.visioncare.com/ask.htm
doctor@visioncare.com

Ask the Optometrist is a question-and-answer service for students, teachers, and parents that provides information about vision, eyes, and eye care. The site also includes a vision FAQ, links to eye care sites, and articles about vision and general eye care.

Ask the Space Scientist

http://image.gsfc.nasa.gov/poetry/ask/askmag.html
odenwald@bolero.gsfc.nasa.gov

Ask the Space Scientist is a question-and-answer service operated by a NASA astronomer. The Space Scientist answers questions about everything having to do with space, including the planets, the solar system, the universe, space travel, and more. The site features an archive of previously answered questions, FAQs, and links to other space-related sites. Ask the Space Scientist is part of the education and public outreach effort of the NASA IMAGE satellite project.

How Things Work

http://landau1.phys.virginia.edu/Education/Teaching/HowThingsWork/home.html
lab3e@virginia.edu

Founded and operated by a physics professor at the University of Virginia, How Things Work is a question-and-answer service for all kinds of physics questions for all ages. The site also features a searchable index of previously-answered questions, a recent questions list, and links to other "How Things Work" resources.

Internet Public Library

http://aristotle.ipl.org/ref/QUE/
iplref@umich.edu

One of several AskA services available through IPL, the Ask-A-Question service will not perform lengthy searches, but will suggest some ideas and resources to help users find the information they seek on virtually any topic. The site also features a FAQ of popular reference questions, a virtual ready reference collection categorized by subject, and tips for searching for information on the Internet as well as in public libraries.

KidsConnect

http://www.ala.org/ICONN/AskKC.html
AskKC@ala.org

KidsConnect is a question answering, help, and referral service for K–12 students on the Internet. The goal of the service is to help students access and use the information available on the Internet effectively and efficiently. KidsConnect is a component of ICONnect, a technology initiative of the American Association of School Librarians (AASL), a division of the American Library Association. KidsConnect is offered in partnership with the Information Institute of Syracuse, Syracuse University, and is underwritten by Microsoft Corporation.

The MAD Scientist Network

http://www.madsci.org
madsci@madsci.wustl.edu

The MAD Scientist Network is composed of over 500 scientists from around the world. The network answers questions in many areas of science and includes an online archive of question-answer sets in addition to other resources. The MAD Scientist Network is operated out of Washington University School of Medicine, St. Louis; funding sources include the Howard Hughes Medical Institute and the Washington University School of Medicine Alumni Association.

Morris County Public Library (New Jersey)

Home Page: *http://www.gti.net/mocolib1/MCL.html*
Query Page: *http://www.gti.net/mocolib1/refbox.html*

Located in Whippany, New Jersey, reference librarians answer all types of questions from the general public and guide non–county residents to services in their area when appropriate.

National Museum of American Art Reference Desk

http://nmaa-ryder.si.edu/referencedesk/
jstahl@nmaa.si.edu

Information specialists at the museum answer questions regarding American art. Specific questions receive brief, factual responses, while users with broad queries are directed to sources to aid in their research. The service is part of the National Museum of American Art of the Smithsonian Institution.

ScienceNet

http://www.sciencenet.org.uk/intro/forms/askaq.html
scienceline@bss.org

ScienceNet is a UK-based question-and-answer service that answers questions in the areas of science, engineering, technology, and medicine. The site includes a keyword-searchable database of previous questions and answers, downloadable BBC radio science broadcasts, interviews with scientists, articles, career information, and more.

References

Allen, B. (1995). Evaluation of reference services. In R. E. Bopp & L. C. Smith (Eds.), *Reference and information services: An introduction* (pp. 207–229). Englewood, CO: Libraries Unlimited.

American Library Association. (1971/1986). *Policy on confidentiality of library records* [Online]. Available: http://www.ala.org/alaorg/oif/pol_conf.html [1998, August 5].

American Library Association. (1995). *American Library Association code of ethics* [Online]. Available: http://www.ala.org/alaorg/oif/ethics.html [1998, August 5].

Arms, C. (1990). Using the national networks: BITNET and the Internet. *Online, 14*(5), 24–29. (EJ 415 245)

Ask a librarian: 13 great websites for grown-ups. (1998, May/June). *Children's Software Revue*, 14.

Balas, J. (1995). The Internet and reference services. *Computers in Libraries, 15*(6), 39–41.

Belkin, N. J. (1980). Anomalous states of knowledge as a basis for information retrieval. *Canadian Journal of Information Science, 5,* 133–143.

Bennett, B. (1997). KidsConnect: Teacher-librarians helping kids solve their information problems on the Internet. *The Teacher Librarian, 4*(3), 14–17.

Bobp, M. E., Kratzert, M., & Richey, D. (1993). The emergence of systemwide electronic access to information sources: The experience of two California State University libraries. *The Reference Librarian, 39,* 111–130.

Branse, Y. (1993). Internet resources: How not to get tangled up in the net. *Bulletin of the Israel Society of Special Libraries and Information Centers, 19*(2), 21–25.

Bry, L. (1997). *Setting up an ask-an-expert service* [Online]. Available: http://www.madsci.org/ask_expert/index.html [1998, July 1].

Bunge, C.A. (1985, Summer). Factors related to reference question answering success: The development of a data-gathering form, *RQ*, 426–86.

Callahan, D. R. (1991). The librarian as change agent in the diffusion of technological innovation. *The Electronic Library, 9*(1), 13–16.

Crews, K. D. (1988, July–September). The accuracy of reference service: Variables for research and implementation. *Library and Information Science Research 10,* 331–55.

Crowley, T. & Childers, T. (1971). *Information service in public libraries: Two studies.* Metuchen, NJ: Scarecrow Press.

Dervin, B., & Nilan M. (1986). Information needs and users. *Annual Review of Information Science and Technology, 21,* 3-31.

Dern, D. P. (1996). Internet: What's next? *InfoWorld* [Online], *18*(27), 66. Available: http://www.infoworld.com/cgi-bin/displayArchive.pl?/96/27/e01-27.65.htm [1998, November 6].

Dick, W., & Carey, L. (1996). *The systematic design of instruction.* 4th ed. New York: HarperCollins.

Feeney, A. (1993). Internet applications: STUMPERS-L. *Computers in Libraries, 13*(5), 40–42.

Foster, S. (1998). *Guide to writing responses* [Online]. Available: http://forum.swarthmore.edu/dr.math/guide/ [1998, August 10].

Gainor, L. & Foster, E. (1993). Usenet and the library. *Reference Services Review, 21*(3), 7–22. (EJ 465 731)

Gustafson, K. L., and Branch, R. M. (1997). *Survey of instructional development models.* 3rd ed. Syracuse, NY: ERIC Clearinghouse on Information & Technology. (ED 411 780)

Hays, C. L. (1997, April 6). Help for the homework challenged. *The New York Times*, 4A pp. 15-16,20.

He, P. W., & Knee, M. (1995). The challenge of electronic services librarianship. *Reference Services Review, 23*(4), 7–12. (EJ 516 526)

Herbst, K. (1995). Webstock '94: Four days of lines and tech talk. *Internet World* [Online], *6*(2), 82. Available: http://www.internetworld.com/print/monthly/1995/02/feat82.htm [1998, November 5].

Hernon, P., & McClure, C. R. (1987). *Unobtrusive testing and library reference service.* Norwood, NJ: Ablex.

Jensen, A., & Sih, J. (1995). Using e-mail and the Internet to teach users at their desktops. *Online 19*(5), 82–86.

Jones, M. K., Li, Z., & Merrill, D. M. (1992). Rapid prototyping in automated instructional design. *ETR&D, 40*(4), 95–100. (EJ 505 459)

Kasowitz, A. (1998). *Guidelines for information specialists of K–12 digital reference services* [Online]. Available: http://www.vrd.org/training/guide.htm [1998, August 5].

Kerka, S. (1996). Distance learning, the Internet, and the World Wide Web. *ERIC Digest*. Columbus: ERIC Clearinghouse on Adult, Career, and Vocational Education. (ED 395 214).

Lankes, R. D. (1995). AskERIC and the virtual library: Lessons for emerging digital libraries. *Internet Research, 5*(1), 56–63. (EJ 505 459)

Lankes, R. D. (1997). Building the Virtual Reference Desk. In *Teaching and Learning in the Digital Age: Research and Practice with Telecommunications in Educational Settings*, ed. Betty Collis and Gerald Knezek, 119-128. Eugene, OR: International Society for Technology in Education.

Lankes, R. D. (1998). *Building and maintaining Internet information services: K–12 digital reference services*. ERIC Clearinghouse on Information and Technology, Syracuse University, Syracuse, NY.

Lankes, R. D., Bry, L., & Whitehead, S. (1996). *The Virtual Reference Desk*. A proposal to the Department of Education. Unpublished proposal, ERIC Clearinghouse on Information and Technology, Syracuse University, Syracuse, NY.

Lewis, D. W. (1995). Traditional reference is dead, now let's move on to important questions. *The Journal of Academic Librarianship, 21*(1), 10–12.

Machovec, G. (1993). VERONICA: A Gopher navigational tool on the Internet. *Online Libraries and Microcomputers, 11*(10), 1–4. (EJ 479 823)

MAD Scientist Network (1997a). *The MadSci moderators' manual* [Online]. Available: http://www.madsci.org/ask_expert/moderators.html [1998, August 10].

MAD Scientist Network (1997b). *The Mad Scientist network: User's manual* [Online]. Available: http://www.madsci.org/ask_expert/exp_manual.html [1998, August 10].

Mardikian, J., & Kesselman, M. (1995). Beyond the desk: Enhanced reference staffing for the electronic library. *Reference Services Review, 23*(1), 21–28. (EJ 498 005)

The Math Forum (1998). *Ask Dr. Math tour: The office* [Online]. Available: http://forum.swarthmore.edu/dr.math/office_help/dr.office_help.html [1998, July 1].

McClure, C. R. (1994). User-based data collection techniques and strategies for evaluating networked information services. *Library Trends, 42*, 591–607. (EJ 489 788)

McClure, C., Moen, W., & Ryan, J. (1994). *Libraries and the Internet/NREN: Perspectives, issues, and challenges.* Westport, CT: Mecklermedia.

Moen, W. (1992). Organizing networked resources for effective use: Classification and other issues in developing navigational tools. *Proceedings of the American Society for Information Science Mid-year Meeting,* 10–21. (EJ 450 404)

Morgan, S. (1995). *Performance assessment in academic libraries.* London: Mansell.

Mullin, M. (1990). *Rapid prototyping for object-oriented systems.* Reading, MA: Addison-Wesley.

Murfin, M. E., & Gugelchuk, G. M. (1987). Development and testing of a reference transaction assessment instrument. *College & Research Libraries, 48,* 314–338. (EJ 357 120)

Romiszowski, A. (1993). Telecommunications and distance education. *ERIC Digest.* Syracuse, NY: ERIC Clearinghouse on Information and Technology. (ED 358 841). (ED 358 841)

Saffo, P. (1994). It's the context, stupid. *Wired, 2*(3), 563–567.

Sanchez, B. & J. Harris, (May 1996). Online mentoring: A success story. *Learning and Leading with Technology, 23,* 57–59. (EJ 526 329)

Saxton, M. L. (1997). Reference service evaluation and meta-analysis: Findings and methodological issues. *The Library Quarterly, 67*(3): 267–289. (EJ 549 329)

Scriven, M. (1991). Efficiency. *Evaluation thesaurus* (4th ed., p. 129). Newbury Park: Sage.

Smith, N. L. & Costello, M. L. (1989). Constructing an operational evaluation design. In D. M. Mertens (Ed.). *Creative ideas for teaching evaluation* (pp. 9-46). Boston, MA: Kluwer Academic Publishers.

Stark, H. (1997). Understanding workflow. In P. Lawrence (Ed.), *Workflow handbook 1997* (pp. 5-25). New York: Wiley.

Still, J., & Campbell, F. (1993). Librarian in a box: The use of electronic mail for reference. *Reference Services Review, 21*(1), 15–18. (EJ 457 878)

Strong, G. E. (1996). Toward a virtual future. In K. Low (Ed.), *The roles of reference librarians: Today and tomorrow* (pp. 153–161). New York: Hawthorn Press.

220

Sutton, S. (1996). Future service models and the convergence of functions: The reference librarian as technician, author and consultant. In K. Low (Ed.), *The roles of reference librarians: Today and tomorrow* (pp. 125–143). New York: Hawthorn Press, and *Reference Librarian, 54*, p.125-143. (EJ 529 662)

System-wide guide to AskERIC question answering. (1998). Unpublished manuscript, ERIC Clearinghouse on Information & Technology, Syracuse University, Syracuse, NY.

Taylor, R. (1968). Question negotiation and information seeking in library. *College & Research Libraries, 29,* 178–194.

Van House, N., Weil, B., & McClure, C. (1990). *Measuring academic library performance: A practical approach.* Chicago: American Library Association.

Wasik, J. M. (1998). *AskA services and funding: An overview* [Online]. Available: http://vrd.org/AskA/aska_funding.html [1998, November 9].

White House. (1997). *Remarks by the President and Mrs. Clinton, the President and Mrs. Bush in presentation of President's Service Awards* [Online]. Available: http://library.whitehouse.gov/cgi-bin/Web_fetch_doc?dataset=Dataset-PressReleases&db=PressReleases&doc_id=7256&query=%23filreq%28%23sum %28volunteerism%29+%23field%28DDATE+%23<>+19970427+19980505%29 %29&use_hyp= [1998, August 5].

White House. (1998). *Vice President Gore praises union efforts to connect 700 of the nation's poorest schools to the Internet* [Online]. Available: http://www.pub.whitehouse.gov/uri-res/I2R?urn:pdi://oma.eop.gov.us/1998/4/28/16.text.1 [1998, December 2].

Bibliography

Annotated ERIC Bibliography

The following journal articles have been indexed and abstracted for the Educational Resources Information Center (ERIC) database.

Abels, E. G. (1996). The e-mail reference interview. *RQ, 35* (3), 345–58. (EJ 526 322)

Discusses differences between e-mail reference interviews and those conducted using other media; presents a taxonomy of approaches to e-mail interviews; and introduces a model e-mail interview, based on a project at the University of Maryland's College of Library and Information Services.

Bushallow-Wilbur, L., DeVinney, G. S., & Whitcomb, F. (1996). Electronic mail reference service: A study. *RQ, 35*, 359–63, 366–71. (EJ 526 323)

Describes a study that examined the use of electronic mail reference service in three library units at the State University of New York at Buffalo. Highlights include patron demographics, question classification, use patterns, and recommendations for further research.

Internet Public Library: Same metaphors, new service. (1997). *American Libraries, 28*(2), 56–59. (EJ 539 658)

A discussion with the staff of the Internet Public Library (IPL), which began as a project at the University of Michigan, highlights its role in supplementing local public library services; classification; collection development policies; and the impact of legislation, copyright, and universal service on IPL. A sidebar presents IPL user statistics.

LaBounty, V. (1997). Reference desk on the Internet. *Book Report, 16*(2), 19. (EJ 550 885)

The KidsConnect service, with 145 volunteers from 39 states and eight countries, connects librarians, teachers, and students with curriculum-related material and other information sources on the Internet. Questions received at the site (on the Web at *http://www.ala.org/ICONN/index.html* or e-mail at *askkc@ala.org*) are routed to volunteer school librarians who respond within 48 hours.

Lankes, R. D. (1995). AskERIC and the virtual library: Lessons for emerging digital libraries. *Internet Research, 5*(1), 56–63. (EJ 505 459)

Explores major issues in creating and maintaining Internet services for AskERIC, an educational digital library started by the Educational Resources Information Center (ERIC) system. Highlights include the importance of user input to shape the service, human intermediaries, AskERIC as a virtual library, future directions, and a copy of the AskERIC brochure.

McKee, M. B. (1995). A day in the life of a virtual librarian. *School Library Journal*, *41*(4), 30–3. (EJ 501 696)

The network information specialists at AskERIC, an Internet-based information service for teachers, library media specialists, administrators, and others involved in education, select and deliver information resources to the information seeker within 48 hours. A sampling of questions and responses is provided in the format of a representative day.

Pack, T. (1996). A guided tour of the Internet Public Library: Cyberspace's unofficial library offers outstanding collections of Internet resources. *Database*, *19*(5), 52–56. (EJ 532 868)

Describes the Internet Public Library, developed at the University of Michigan's School of Information and Library Studies. Site highlights include the reference center; the reading room, which includes materials in full-text; youth and teen services; professional information for librarians; links to Web search engines; a Multiuser Object Oriented (MOO) reference area; and a virtual exhibit hall.

Ryan, S. (1996). Reference service for the Internet community: A case study of the Internet Public Library Reference Division. *Library & Information Science Research*, *18*(3), 241–59. (EJ 532 939)

Examines the creation of the Internet Public Library Reference Division in the historical context of librarians' efforts to integrate the use of technologies with reference services. Discussion considers ways that librarians have successfully incorporated new technologies and makes recommendations for use of the Reference Division and Internet usage for the reference process in general.

Serving the Internet public: The Internet Public Library. (1996). *Electronic Library*, *14*(2), 122–26. (EJ 526 267)

Describes the Internet Public Library (IPL), which was developed at the School of Information and Library Studies at the University of Michigan to be a library for Internet users. Highlights include mission statement and goals, funding, staffing with volunteers, future possibilities, IPL services, and statement of principles.

Still, J., & Campbell, F. (1993). Librarian in a box: The use of electronic mail for reference. *Reference Services Review*, *21*(1), 15–18. (EJ 457 878)

Discusses the use of electronic mail for reference services and investigates systems in health sciences libraries and in academic libraries. The use of electronic mail for services including interlibrary loan, online search requests, literature searches, photocopies or other document delivery, reference questions, and purchase requests is described.

Tobiason, K. (1997). Taking by giving: KidsConnect and your media center. *Technology Connection, 4*(6), 10–11. (EJ 554 221)

> Discusses KidsConnect (KC), an initiative of the American Association of School Librarians (AASL), volunteer service to help children access and use the information available on the Internet effectively and efficiently. Describes the benefits to volunteers: improved Internet skills; knowledge of Internet-related resources; familiarity with worthwhile educational Web sites; collegial support; the thrill of information seeking and retrieval; and professional renewal.

How to Order ERIC Documents

Individual copies of ERIC documents are available in either microfiche or paper copy from the ERIC Document Reproduction Service (EDRS), 7420 Fullerton Road, Suite 110, Springfield, VA 22153-2852; some are available only in microfiche. Information needed for ordering includes the ED number, the number of pages, the number of copies wanted, the unit price, and the total unit cost. Sales tax should be included on orders from Maryland, Virginia, and Washington, DC.

Please order by ED number, indicate the format desired (microfiche or paper copy), and include payment for the price listed plus shipping. Call EDRS at 1-800-443-ERIC (or 703-440-1400) or e-mail EDRS customer service department: *service@edrs.com*, for information on pricing, shipping costs and/or other services offered by the contractor.

Inquiries about ERIC may be addressed to the ERIC Clearinghouse on Information & Technology, 4-194 Center for Science and Technology, Syracuse University, Syracuse, NY 13244-4100 (800-464-9107), e-mail: *eric@ericir.syr.edu*; or ACCESS ERIC, 2277 Research Boulevard, 7A, Rockville, MD 20850 (800-LET-ERIC), e-mail: *acceric@inet.ed.gov*

Journal Articles

Copies of journal articles can be found in library periodical collections; through interlibrary loan; from the journal publisher; or from article reprint services such as the UMI/InfoStore (1-800-248-0360), UnCover Company (1-800-787-7979), or Institute for Scientific Information (ISI) (1-800-336-4474). Information needed for ordering includes the author, title of article, name of journal, volume, issue number, page numbers, date, and EJ number for each article. Fax services are available.

Non-ERIC Documents

The following documents have been selected by the Virtual Reference Desk Project as a subset of the current literature on digital reference and AskA services. The documents are divided into separate categories to represent different contexts of digital reference: digital reference and AskA services and business (digital reference as customer support).

Digital Reference and AskA Services

Bennett, B. A. (1997). KidsConnect: Teacher-librarians helping kids solve their information problems on the Internet. *The Teaching Librarian, 4*(3), 14–17.

Frank, I. B. (1998). E-mail reference service at the University of South Florida: A well-kept secret. *Art Documentation, 17*(1), 8–9, 44. (Revision of a talk given at the 1997 ARLIS/NA Conference.)

Fishman, D. L. (1998). Managing the virtual reference desk: How to plan an effective reference e-mail system. *Medical Reference Services Quarterly, 17*(1), 1–10. (Presented at the University of Maryland Health Sciences Library; based on a presentation at the 1996 MLA Conference.)

Lankes, R. D. (1993). AskERIC: The virtual librarian. *Information Searcher, 6*(1), 20–2.

Lagace, N. (1998). The Internet Public Library's "Ask a question worldwide reference service." *Art Documentation, 17*(1), 5–7. (Revision of a talk given at the 1997 ARLIS/NA Conference.)

Lessick, S., Kjaer, K., & Clancy, S. (1997). *Interactive Reference Service (IRS) at UC Irvine: Expanding reference service beyond the reference desk* [Online]. Available: http://www.ala.org/acrl/paperhtm/a10.html (Accessed August 5, 1998).

Lipow, A. G. (1997). Thinking out loud: Who will give reference service in the digital environment? *Reference & User Services Quarterly, 37*(2), 125–29.

Ormes, S. (1998). Feature: Ask a librarian. *Library Technology* [Online], *3*(2). Available: http://www.sbu.ac.uk/litc/lt/1998/news619.html (Accessed 31 July 1998).

Sloan, B. (1997). *Service perspectives for the digital library: Remote reference services* [Online]. Available: http://www.lis.uiuc.edu/~sloan/e-ref.html (Accessed July 21, 1998).

Stahl, J. R. (1998). 'Have a question? Click here': Electronic reference at the National Museum of American Art. *Art Documentation, 17*(1), 10–12. (Revision of a talk given at the ARLIS/NA Conference.)

Summers, R. (1998). Meeting education information needs through digital reference. *Art Documentation, 17*(1): 3–4, 68. (Regarding AskERIC and KidsConnect; revision of a talk given at the 1997 ARLIS/NA Conference.)

Tillman, H. N. (1990). Electronic reference service on Jumbonet. In *IOLS '90, Integrated Online Library Systems* (231–236). Medford, NJ: Learned Information.

Business: Digital Reference as Customer Support

Kay, A. S. (1997, December 8). Call centers meet the Web. *LAN Times, 14*(25), 41–42.

Nelson, M. (1998, June 8). Trio looks to customer service. *InfoWorld, 20*(23), 63.

O'Connell, P. L. (1998, July 6). We got your e-mail; Just don't expect a reply. *The New York Times*, p. D3.

Sterne, J. (1998, May 1). Minding the mail. *CIO Web Business*, 30, 32.

What is ERIC?

ERIC, the Educational Resources Information Center, is a national education information system sponsored by the Office of Educational Research and Improvement in the U.S. Department of Education. The main product of ERIC is a bibliographic database containing citations and abstracts for over 950,000 documents and journal articles published since 1966. Most of the document literature cited in ERIC can be read in full text at any of the 900+ libraries or institutions worldwide holding the ERIC microfiche collection. In addition, users can purchase copies of ERIC documents from the ERIC Document Reproduction Service. Journal articles cited in ERIC can be obtained at a subscribing library, through interlibrary loan, or from an article reprint service

How do I find information in ERIC?

The ERIC Database can be searched manually through its two print indexes, Resources in Education (RIE) and Current Index to Journals in Education (CIJE). Over 3,000 libraries and information centers subscribe to one or both of these monthly indexes. The database can also be searched online: (a) through a computer based information retrieval service; (b) by CD-ROM; (c) on a locally mounted system, which may be accessible through the Internet; or (d) Internet: http://ericir.syr.edu/Eric/. The number of libraries offering online and CD-ROM search services is rapidly increasing.

What is ERIC/IT?

The ERIC Clearinghouse on Information & Technology, or ERIC/IT, is one of 16 clearinghouses in the ERIC system. It specializes in library and information science and educational technology. ERIC/IT acquires, selects, catalogs, indexes, and abstracts documents and journal articles in these subject areas for input into the ERIC database. Among the topics covered in library and information science are:

- management, operation, and use of libraries and information centers
- library technology and automation
- library education
- information policy
- information literacy
- information storage, processing and retrieval
- networking

Topics covered in educational technology include:
- design, development, and evaluation of instruction
- computer-assisted instruction
- hypermedia, interactive video, and interactive multimedia
- telecommunications
- film, radio, television, and other audio-visual media
- distance education
- simulation and gaming

What is available from ERIC/IT?

Each year, ERIC/IT publishes Monographs, Digests, and Minibibliographies in the fields of educational technology and library and information science. Our semiannual newsletter, ERIC/IT Update, announces new clearinghouse products and developments, and ERIC/IT Networkers provide helpful information for using ERIC-related resources on the Internet.

Publications

- Digests, providing brief overviews of topics of current interest and references for further reading
- Monographs, featuring trends and issues analyses, synthesis papers and annotated bibliographies
- ERIC/IT Update, a semi-annual newsletter

User Services

- Response to inquiries about ERIC and matters within the ERIC/IT scope area
- Workshops and presentations about ERIC and database searching
- Assistance in searching the ERIC database

AskERIC

- Internet-based question answering service for educators
- AskERIC Virtual Library, an Internet site of education-related information resources including lesson plans, InfoGuides, listservs and much more
    E-mail: *askeric@askeric.org*
    Internet: *http://www.askeric.org*

Would you like to submit your work to ERIC?

Have you written materials related to educational technology or library and information science that you would like to share with others? ERIC/IT would be interested in reviewing your work for possible inclusion in the ERIC database. We actively solicit documents from researchers, practitioners, associations, and agencies at national, state, and local levels. ERIC documents include the following and more:

- Research Reports
- Program Descriptions
- Instructional Materials
- Conference Papers
- Teaching Guides
- Opinion Papers

How do I find out more?

For additional information about ERIC or about submitting documents, or for a current publications list, contact:

ERIC Clearinghouse on Information & Technology
4-194 Center for Science and Technology
Syracuse University
Syracuse, New York 13244-4100
R. David Lankes, Director
Telephone: (315) 443-3640   Fax: (315) 443-5448   (800) 464-9107
E-mail: *eric@ericir.syr.edu*   WWW URL: *http://ericir.syr.edu/ithome*

Questions about the ERIC system can also be directed to:

ACCESS ERIC
2277 Research Boulevard, 7A
Rockville, Maryland 20850
Telephone: (800) LET-ERIC
Internet: *acceric@inet.ed.gov*
             http://www.aspensys.com/eric/

ERIC Clearinghouses
- Adult, Career, and Vocational Education
- Assessment and Evaluation
- Community Colleges
- Counseling and Student Services
- Disabilities and Gifted Education
- Educational Management
- Elementary and Early Childhood Education
- Higher Education
- Information & Technology
- Languages and Linguistics
- Reading, English, and Communication
- Rural Education and Small Schools
- Science, Mathematics, and Environmental Education
- Social Studies/Social Science Education
- Teaching and Teacher Education
- Urban Education

Support Components

- ERIC Document Reproduction Service
   Telephone: (800) 443-ERIC (3742)
- ERIC Processing and Reference Facility
   Telephone: (800) 799-ERIC (3742)

Appendix A

AskA Service Blueprints

Each AskA service in this section is presented as a blueprint. These blueprints serve as both examples of how plans can be structured and cases that can be emulated. The full method for developing these blueprints, as well as more complete, standardized descriptions of each service, can be found in the companion study to this Starter Kit, *Building and Maintaining Internet Information Services: K–12 Digital Reference Services* (Lankes, 1998).

The Blueprint Metaphor

The framework of detectors, rules, and effectors presented in Module 2 organizes the multiple ideas and data from the planning process into transferable sets of detectors, rules, resources, and effectors. Just as an architect's blueprint can describe a rich, multidimensional construction of a building in a transferable way, these blueprints capture the multifaceted digital reference service into a succinct, transferable description.

However, as with architectural blueprints, there are limitations to these empirically based descriptions. These service blueprints identify that a feature (descriptor, rule, effector) is present, but not *why* it is present. Further, these descriptions do not capture the dynamic nature of the service development process in the sense that they do not show how rules, detectors, and effectors came into being or change over time. They do indicate any iterative functions that exist in the service as presently structured.

The blueprints can be read left to right, with the leftmost column listing detector information. These detectors are segmented vertically by agent types from the conceptual framework (users, information services, application builders, infrastructure providers, internal, and external). An agent type will not be listed if it is not used. Certain detectors are marked as "Key Detectors." These are detectors upon which the organization relies as the most important information sources when building and maintaining its service. Certain detectors are connected to processes in place at the service. These are the rules used to process detector information and produce effectors. Effectors are marked in black with white type. Each component of the blueprint (detector, rule component, effector) can have one or more resources associated with it. Resources are physical mechanisms or component mechanisms used at a certain point in the process. Figure 2-2 graphically depicts the structure of the blueprint.

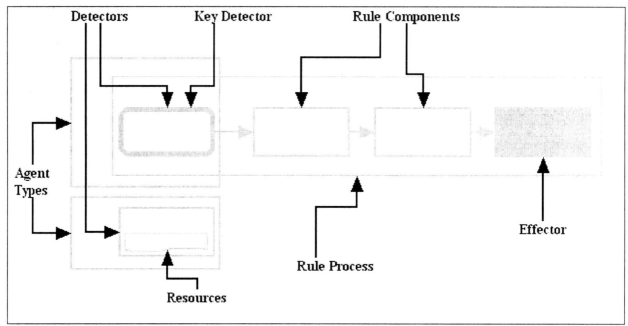

Figure A-1 Structure of Blueprints

The following pages contain blueprints of three exemplary AskA services: Ask Dr. Math, the National Museum of American Art Reference Desk, and the MAD Scientist Network. See Module 2 for case studies of each of these services.

These and other blueprint figures may be seen in full size at URL: *http://ericir.syr.edu/ithome/bmiis*

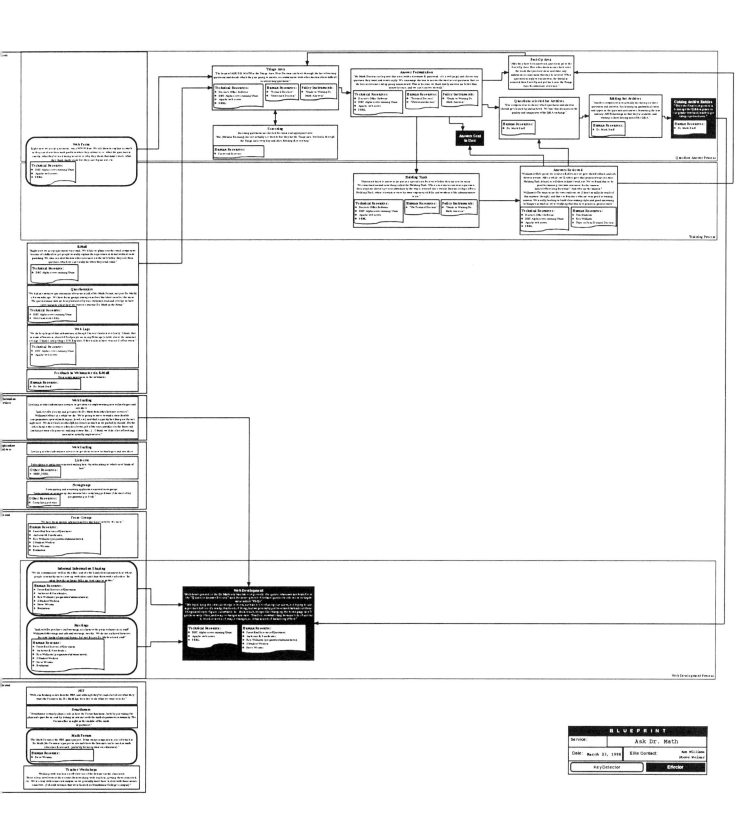

BLUEPRINT

Service: Ask Dr. Math

Date: March 23, 1998

Elite Contact: Ken Williams
Steve Weimar

KeyDetector   Effector

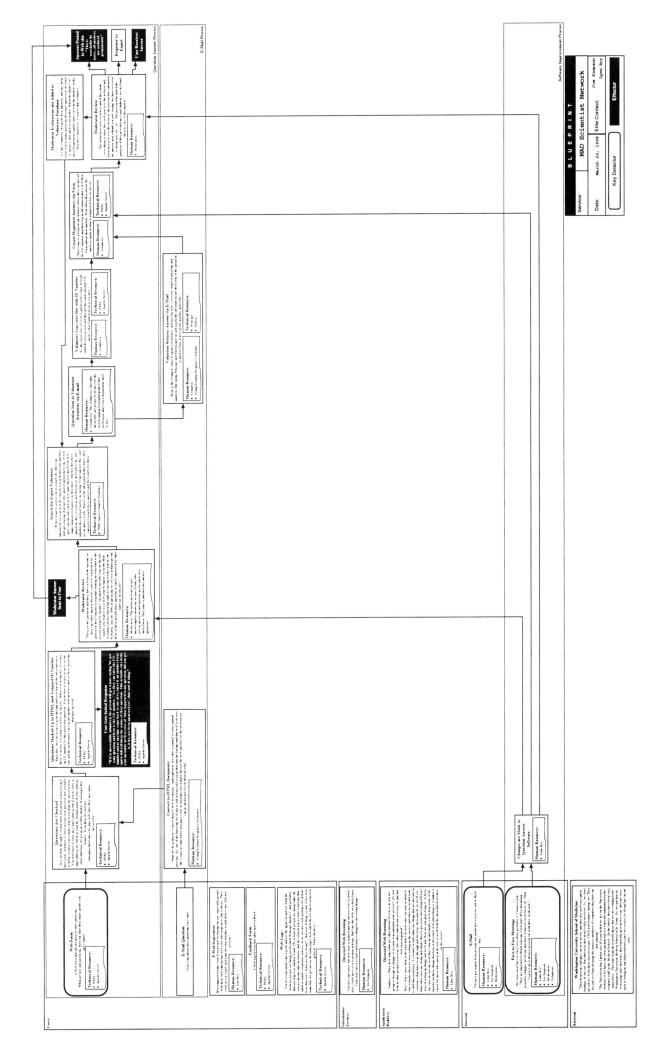

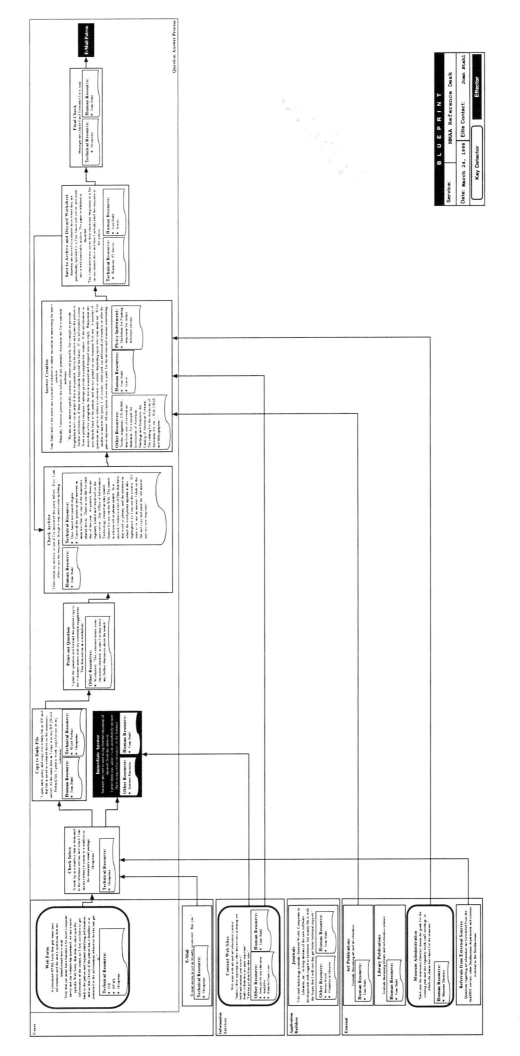